32 Laps

32 Laps

TIPPING POINTS THAT MOTIVATE CHANGE

AND IDENTIFY MEANING IN YOUR BUSINESS AND IN YOUR LIFE

Michael C. Fling, D.D.S.

Advantage.

Published by Advantage, Charleston, South Carolina.
Member of Advantage Media Group.

ADVANTAGE is a registered trademark and the Advantage colophon is a trademark of Advantage Media Group, Inc.

Printed in the United States of America.

ISBN: 978-159932-367-1
LCCN: 2012956013

This publication is designed to provide accurate and authoritative information in regard to the subject matter covered. It is sold with the understanding that the publisher is not engaged in rendering legal, accounting, or other professional services. If legal advice or other expert assistance is required, the services of a competent professional person should be sought.

 Advantage Media Group is proud to be a part of the Tree Neutral® program. Tree Neutral offsets the number of trees consumed in the production and printing of this book by taking proactive steps such as planting trees in direct proportion to the number of trees used to print books. To learn more about Tree Neutral, please visit www.treeneutral.com. To learn more about Advantage's commitment to being a responsible steward of the environment, please visit www.advantagefamily.com/green

Advantage Media Group is a leading publisher of business, motivation, and self-help authors. Do you have a manuscript or book idea that you would like to have considered for publication? Please visit www.advantagefamily.com or call 1.866.775.1696

"It is not in the knowing;
it is in the doing."

—Michael C. Fling, D.D.S.

Acknowledgments

I still remember growing up in east Dallas, Texas. We didn't have a lot, but we also never went without. As I reflect, it wasn't the things we did or didn't have that really mattered.

Rather, it was the development and values that my parents instilled in me that gave me such direction. Not that I always needed a push. Their gift was to give me freedom and to trust and support my dreams any way they could. They gave priority to family, as I still treasure eating the special dinners cooked by my grandfather Pappy while watching the Dallas Cowboys. It was so much fun watching Pappy curse the referees. To him, refs and Republicans were evil. I thank my mom and dad for creating such great memories.

As I started my career in dentistry, there were two giants in our profession who believed in me: Dr. Herb Shillingberg and Dr. Jim Kessler. Much like my parents, they gave me the freedom to grow, or sometimes they gave me just enough rope that I didn't hurt myself. I will always be in debt to them for the faith they placed in me and for the many opportunities to make a difference.

And then there is my lab technician and good friend, Jeff. That sounds crazy, doesn't it? My lab guy? Jeff Singler has been my best friend since second grade. Thick or thin, he is there. While his lab work is extraordinary, his heart and compassion is even more so. There are only a few people in the world you can claim as close friends. Jeff is such a friend for me, and he has inspired me my entire life.

As my practice and business grew, I heard of a dentist in Oklahoma City named Dr. Bill Lockard. Based on all I had heard, I thought he could walk on water. I had the good fortune to purchase his practice in 1990. The personal and professional growth he ignited within me is beyond anything I can easily express. His mentorship has gone well beyond dentistry and for that I am grateful. He has become a second father to me.

Dr. Lockard solidified my involvement with an educational facility in Key Biscayne, Florida, known as the Pankey Institute. Dr. Pankey was a dentist who had such a profound impact on people and dental practices that an institution was developed to teach the technical, managerial, and philosophical tenets that had made him so remarkable. These tenets are applicable to any person and any business. Although Dr. Pankey passed away several years ago, many people have played a significant role in continuing to foster those tenets at the Pankey Institute. Even I have played a minor role in that process. I cannot think of one entity in dentistry that has played as significant a role in the lives of dentists and their patients as the Pankey Institute.

During my professional journey I crossed paths with another leader who has given me abundant opportunities to touch the lives of many people. Dr. Michael Cowen is the founder of the Seattle Study Clubs. He has developed a remarkable network of clubs dedicated to personal and professional growth. He and his team have truly changed the face of dentistry. I owe him and his entire team a debt of gratitude for affording me amazing opportunities and for allowing me to play a small role in changing so many lives.

One day I met a young practice consultant who had really big dreams. While he couldn't yet walk on water, he had a clear vision for just that. Kirk Behrendt has become a dear and inspiring friend. The trust and mentorship he has placed in me warms my heart. Together, Kirk and I have developed our own clear vision for changing the world together—not just the dentists we consult but people from every walk of life. It is the vision that he and I developed many years ago that has inspired me to write this book. Many thanks, Kirk, for your special gifts.

I must mention one thing that I often take for granted, yet it has the most meaning in my life: my family. I simply cannot express the magnitude of the gratitude and the love I hold for my children, Tyler and Kinsey, and my wife, Leslie. They are the reason I exist. The times we have spent together in play and at work have created wonderful memories. Watching football games while eating spaghetti and meatballs cooked from the recipe Pappy passed along to us are special times. I believe my children are very special in their own unique way. I have no doubt they too can give back to the world in a way that has meaning. And the anchor of it all is my wife, Leslie. How she has managed to balance our business, raise two children (and another kid at heart—me), and still have the tenacity to love me, in spite of me, is amazing. I don't want to imply it has been easy. It has not. But nothing worthwhile is easy. As you are about to learn, I have never doubted her clarity when it comes to the love she has for our children and for me. That is the glue that holds my world together.

Table of Contents

Warm Up

"It is not in the knowing;
it is in the doing."

*I*t was the fall of 2010 when I was motivated to get in better shape. I had lifted weights with a buddy for many years, but I didn't do much aerobic activity. As a matter of fact, my favorite aerobic activity was eating. Not to say that I was grossly overweight or out of shape—I wasn't. But I now had the motivation to do more. I don't remember how, but I was exposed to swimming. I had never done much swimming and as I began my efforts, I felt defeated when, upon my first attempt, I was able to swim only one and a half laps. I wondered how I would ever complete the thirty-two laps that made a mile. I knew how to swim, but swimming for an entire mile, that was another story.

"Don't tell me what you are going to do; tell me what you have done." I have passed that adage along to my children on a regular basis. I started my career in my teens, when I was trained as a dental laboratory technician, and I progressed through dental school. I now practice as a restorative dentist. Early in my career, I was given the opportunity to teach at our local dental school, where even twenty-eight years later I still actively contribute some of my time and energy.

As a matter of fact, my opportunity to teach other dentists and their teams has grown beyond my wildest dreams. I have been named by *Dentistry Today* as one of the Top 100 Clinicians in Dental Education every year since 2005. I have had the good fortune to speak to groups around the world and in the United States on technical and motivational topics. As with almost any business or service company, there are different ways to provide care and there are different levels of quality and expertise. I often teach a technique or a basic fundamental concept only to have the student or dentist say, "I already know that." When I evaluate what that person actually does, I learn that it is very different from what that person knows. I believe that one of the keys to success is bridging the gap between knowing and doing.

> **One of the keys to success** is bridging the gap between knowing and doing.

This is especially true in dentistry, where thirty-two is a kind of magic number. Most of us have thirty-two permanent adult teeth. To a dentist, each tooth can convey a lesson of lasting value, something we gain first by being trained to know the problem we face, then by doing something about it. The thirty-two lessons each tooth gives corresponds to the thirty-two lessons in this book—lessons that teach us that the gap between knowing and doing can have lasting significance.

Think of all of the examples that demonstrate the disconnect between knowing and doing that could make such a difference in the world around us. We know that driving while impaired can be devastat-

One of the
keys to success
is bridging the gap between
knowing and doing.

ing, yet one person is killed every half-hour due to drunk driving, and over 16,000 are killed in alcohol-related crashes every year. This comprises almost half of all traffic fatalities. While we know the risk of drinking and driving, many still drink and drive. The intent usually isn't to be malicious.

> To a dentist, each tooth corresponds to the thirty-two lessons in this book—lessons that teach us that the gap between knowing and doing can have lasting significance.

There are so many other factors that can contribute to this tragedy. But the fact is that there is a disconnect between knowing and doing.

We know that many disease processes are affected by smoking. Yet almost 21 percent of the US population smokes—that is 44.5 million people. This equates to over $160 billion in smoking-related health costs. Approximately half a million people die each year in the USA due to smoking.

While most know the ramifications of this habit, there are obviously many factors that relate to the actions people take or don't take, that affect what they do. While many would choose not to have bad habits or addictions, we have to wonder what prevents us from changing our behavior. There is a disconnect between knowing and doing. So we must consider what factors can motivate us to act differently even when it is not easy.

> Another key to success is to find the disconnect between knowing and doing.

Warm-up Lesson: *My son Tyler was in finals at college. All of our family members have become big basketball fans of the Oklahoma City Thunder. Having a pro franchise like the Thunder in our city has been amazing. When one of the playoff games was the night before his final exam, he "knew" that it was more important to study for his exam than to attend the game. It took some insistence from his dad that what he should do was study and not attend the game. The disconnect between knowing and doing can be a challenge to overcome. It is not always easy.*

There are many factors that can lead to action. One of the keys to bridging the gap between knowing and doing is to "put it on the shelf." When I started my business of Fling Seminars, I was compelled to stimulate, educate, and inspire dentists and their teams to success. I knew what I wanted to do, but I wasn't sure how to do it.

My good friend and colleague Kirk Behrendt gave me some advice that sent me on my way. He said the first thing I had to do was to "put it on the

> There are many factors that can lead to action. One of the keys to bridging the gap between knowing and doing is to "put it on the shelf."

shelf." I wasn't sure exactly what he meant. He was saying that first I had to develop my presentation. I had to get it together and have it ready. I had to have it on the shelf. Then, when I had the opportunity, I had the material and content ready to present. When I received my first invitation to speak, I already had the seminar together. Now it was up to me to present it in a way that was stimulating and relevant.

I have said as long as I have been a teacher, "The fundamentals have not changed. It isn't what you know that will make the difference. It is applying what you already know." It is not in the knowing; it is in the doing. It is that difference that can improve the quality of your life and the life of those around you.

"The fundamentals have not changed. It isn't what you know that will make the difference. It is applying what you already know."

As you explore *Thirty-Two Laps*, I hope you will have insight into many of the people and lessons that have guided my path and inspired me not just to know but to also do. I hope you will find that one thing that can motivate you to change. See why completing those thirty-two laps became so important to me and use that inspiration to make a positive change in your life or in the life of those around you. Study each lap and you will find a lesson that can lead you to a better place: **the Tipping Point that motivates change.**

Lap 1
It All Starts Here

So I wanted to swim a mile. That is a long way—thirty-two laps, to be exact—and I quickly found that to swim only two laps was hard enough. I had to pack the gym bag and remember my goggles, earplugs, and a fashionable swimsuit was imperative. The hardest thing for me was getting into the pool. That water is cold. And for someone who was new at swimming, a mile was a challenge that absolutely required me to work my way up to that distance. Oh, to be young again.

I had to schedule a dedicated practice time and develop the intent to succeed. I had to prepare my day and be willing to work hard even on the days that my mind and body were not in agreement with my heart. So what is it that motivated me to work so hard and to eventually achieve that distance? What was one of the key factors that motivated me to swim a mile? First, I had to develop a new clarity—the clarity of a healthier me. It may sound crazy, but as I would swim each lap, I would picture a healthier me. Health became a compelling issue. That was a huge part of the inspiration to swim.

> **I had to develop a new clarity.**

Swimming not only expanded my mental picture of a healthier me but it also gave me a time and place to reflect on the past. I found that mental images of both my past memories and the future of a healthier me were compelling enough to inspire change. I would reflect on my youth and on happy times from my past. Those memories gave me reason to love life even more. That fueled my passion and intent and pushed me to go farther. Then I would project images of a healthier me. I would envision a stronger me. My clear vision of my past and future was what compelled me to swim. I could do this!

> I found that mental images of both my past memories and the future of a healthier me were compelling enough to inspire change.

Think about this just a minute. Why we do things can be boiled down into a few simple reasons.

We do things:

1. To preserve ourselves or to help preserve others, or
2. To preserve or elevate our self-esteem or to improve the self-esteem of others.

Let me share with you an example of how this can affect action. I have discussions with my patients not only about their dental health but also about their health in general. It is interesting to see how

Why do we do the things we do?

1. To preserve ourselves or to help preserve others, or...

2. To preserve or elevate our self-esteem or to improve the self-esteem of others.

smoking produces so many of the clinical symptoms that I observe. As I visit with smokers, I ask why they began to smoke. Often, it was because, when they were young or in college, it was "the thing to do" with their friends. Said another way, they began to smoke because of peer pressure or to fit in; it elevated their self-esteem.

Lap 1 Lesson: *We make decisions and we act to preserve our self or help preserve others. Said another way, we do what we do in an effort to survive or to help others survive. This can be as basic as food and water to as complex as helping a broken heart.* **We must survive before we thrive.** *Beyond that, we act so that we can feel better about ourselves, or so that we can help someone feel better about himself or herself.*

The fact is that most of these people I talk to want to quit or have already tried unsuccessfully to quit. There is no doubt that smoking is a habit that has a tight grip on many; many feel the physical addiction. I have found it equally interesting that when some smokers develop cancer, they find the inspiration to quit smoking cold turkey after having been completely unsuccessful many times before. What is different now that they have found their "tipping point"? What has motivated them to change?

> ## Their desire to preserve themselves has taken over.

Their desire to preserve themselves has taken over. The desire to survive has created such inspiration that quitting can occur.

Reflecting on past memories gives you the passion to live; developing mental images of a future healthier you, recognizing that self-esteem is not related to this habit, and attempting to preserve yourself, these past and future mental images can provide a tipping point that motivates you to make a positive change. This is where taking action to quit begins. The real trick is to recognize the tipping point for change before your actions have negative consequences.

> The real trick is to recognize the tipping point for change before your actions have negative consequences.

It was the development of a clear vision of a healthier me that helped bridge the gap between my *knowing* that exercise was beneficial and actually doing the exercise. Then my health benefited from swimming. It wasn't that I didn't know that exercise was important, but it was finding meaningful inspiration that caused me to act. I had to find a good reason to lower myself into that cold water every day.

It's not in the knowing; it is in the doing. I began to

> It's not in the knowing; it is in the doing.

eliminate the disconnect between knowing and doing by developing mental pictures of a new, healthier me, and by reflecting on memories that inspired me to live life to the fullest and with intent.

Lap 1 Tipping Point
Develop your clarity and use past and present mental images to compel positive action.

Lap 2
Fearless Clarity

I have had many hobbies in the past. I have been accused of being an adrenaline addict. Anything you can do that is on the edge, that is what I enjoy. White-water kayaking, aerobatic flying, and driving race cars are a few examples of my kind of fun. Now understand, I enjoy these things as long as I am the one in control. When my son Tyler was ten, he and I started racing karts. These were not ordinary karts. These were high-tech bullets that could accelerate to over 100 mph before you said go. Of course, we had to move on to bigger and better things, so we moved into racing a formula car.

These cars are not like something you'd see in a NASCAR event. Rather, these are open-wheel cars of the kind you see in the Indy 500. They are not nearly as fast or sophisticated as a true Indy car, but even so, an absolute handful for me. If you have never been up close and personal to a formula car, let me explain some things about the car and my experience.

Not far from our house is a road course called Hallett Racing Circuit. It is a 1.8-mile road course that has ten turns and more than eighty feet of elevation change. It is a technically demanding course.

One dewy morning we were testing our new car, hoping to find a setup that would make us fast. When you sit in a formula car, you almost lie down. It is not quiet, but you are tucked in pretty snugly in a reclined position. A seat is made for you that is molded along your back so that you have a secure and customized fit inside the cockpit. The steering wheel is removable, and a computer is mounted on it so that you can easily reference all of the parameters of the car. The gearshift handle is positioned just next to your right hand. Your feet rest close together with a clutch, brake, and gas pedal also very close together. It is important to be able to work two of the foot pedals with one foot at the same time. This means that walking and chewing gum at the same time is a prerequisite. I use sugar-free gum.

In the event the car should flip over—keeping in mind it is an open-cockpit car—your forearms are strapped into the car, preventing them from escaping beyond the cockpit. You wear fire-retardant socks, shoes, underwear, head sock, race suit, and gloves.

Needless to say, the 100-degree day you sit strapped in the car, waiting patiently on the grid to go out on track, is a day that you are soaked in perspiration. Your helmet fits firmly on your head and you wear a neck-restraint unit, called a Hans device, around your neck. It is contoured to rest over the top of your shoulders and it goes behind your head. It sticks up behind the back of your helmet. It has straps that extend to clip on to either side of the helmet. There are six seat belts that firmly hold you in place. Two belts come under/between your legs, two come around your hips at your waist, and two come down over the top of your shoulders and the Hans device. Your arm belts are integrated to connect with the shoulder belts. All six belts meet in the middle of the waist and are connected together with a "quick disconnect" near your belly button.

In the event you need to exit the car fast, the quick disconnect is activated and all of the belts are released. The arm belts release too and the steering wheel comes off. Easy. The concept of the Hans unit is such that if the car smacks head-on into a wall, the device prevents your head and neck from jerking forward as the impact stops the car. This prevents your noggin from separating from the rest of you. Could this device have saved Dale Earnhardt's life?

Focus with a fearless clarity.

Today, this device is a must when you are on the track. Head and body movement are limited. The snug fit in the car makes the space your personal cocoon. Because you recline, the ability to see over the nose of the car is not possible.

Now I'm set. It is time to go fast. I exit the pits on this dewy morning and proceed down a long straightaway. I have some concerns about track grip as the track seems a little damp from the fog and dew. As I enter the track, I notice a sharp, burning sensation in my right leg, but I focus because it is time to go fast. This is the fastest part of the track.

As my speed approaches 120 mph, the noise is loud. My helmet visor is fogging in the morning air, impairing my ability to see. So I crack my visor open a little to let the wind come inside the helmet and disperse the fog. The noise becomes even louder. As I approach the hard left-hander, I use my brake and clutch while dropping down to second gear. I brake with the toe of my right foot while managing the gas pedal with the heel of the same foot. I notice the front tires starting to smoke. I have too much brake pressure on the front brakes. I reach for a knob on the right side of the cockpit, and I turn it a half-turn to the left. That affects the brake bias and transfers the brake pressure from the front tires to rear tires.

I focus because it is time to go fast. Out of this corner, I have to set up for a long right-hander. Around a slower car and up the hill I go. I shift to fourth gear. As I set up for the turn, I cannot understand what someone is trying to tell me from the pits. I have a radio in my car that plugs into the speakers in my helmet. There is a microphone mounted inside my helmet too. I press the push-to-talk switch on the steering wheel while turning right at almost 100 mph. I ask, "What did you say?" I still cannot understand what he is saying.

Through two left-handers, I drive up the hill to the most difficult part of the track, called the Bitch. You can imagine why it is named that name. It isn't easy. I top the hill, which has a blind corner just over the top. It is important to be on the gas hard as you top this blind part of the track. If you let off the gas here, you will lose rear-tire grip in the corner and surely spin out the car. Fast over the hill and then quickly down the other side to a sharp right-hander. It was then that I understood what my pit crew was frantically trying to tell me. "There is a wreck in the Bitch!" As I top the hill I brake hard and down-shift from fifth to second. A car sits in the middle of the right turn. I let off the brakes and veer wide left to avoid hitting the stalled car. My left tires go off into the dirt, but I pass safely around. I focus. It is time to go fast. Up the hill to the final set of left-handers.

My computer starts to flash "temperature." Now I have to be concerned with overheating and damaging the engine. I negotiate the turns and pass the start-finish line with the warning still flashing. Wow! I'm worn out.

Now think about all that was going on. The track grip was a question. I couldn't see, the noise is roaring, the brakes need adjusting, my pit crew is talking to me, trying to warn me of an accident, and my engine temperature is too high. All of this, plus I have to drive the car on a very demanding track to the fastest of my ability without spinning out.

In spite of all of those things, guess what happened on that lap? I set a new track record for our class of car. I was fired up. In all honesty, the record was broken only a few minutes later by a friend in a formula car that was even faster. But at least I had the glory for a brief minute. Now think about it. If you are a fan in the stands watching that lap, it seems pretty boring and uneventful. It is a car going around the track. It

There is a complexity to simplicity.

seems simple. But you know that isn't the case. There are so many things going on at once. There is a complexity to simplicity. While completing the lap may appear simple, there are a multitude of things going on all at one time that make it very complex. It is having a keen focus that ignores fear while keeping the end in mind that allows success. It is having the clarity to know that I am going to go fast regardless of the obstacles ahead.

Lap 2 Lesson: *We have to evaluate, process, and react to a barrage of external factors that come at us in ways that we never expected. So what helps us succeed? It starts by having not just clarity but a fearless clarity and mental image with the end in our mind.*

It is critical that I respect the challenges ahead. But my meticulous preparation and focus supersedes my fear. Having a fearless clarity inspires me to meticulously prep the car, to refine my driving skills, and to attempt to anticipate the unexpected. I have the mental image and focus to overcome any of the obstacles ahead. My job is to prepare and perform so well that I make the complex seem simple. Making something difficult more manageable begins with having fearless clarity.

Lap 2 Tipping Point
Respect challenges ahead but create actions that are derived from meticulous preparation and a focus that supersedes fear.

Respect challenges ahead

but create actions

that are derived from

meticulous preparation

and a focus that

supersedes fear.

Lap 3

Expect the Unexpected

~~~~~~

O h, by the way, do you remember that burning sensation that was in my leg as I left the pits in the race car? That was a pen I had left in my pocket. Ouch. You see, even when we plan to be our best, things may not always go as planned. We have to expect the unexpected. Our business is often like the record lap I just completed. We have to be willing to accept all of the external factors that we never

> We have to give our customers the impression that what is complex is simple, so that they can trust our actions.

expected and perform in spite of the obstacles. The audience sitting in the stands, watching the race—or our customers—often cannot appreciate the complexity of our mission. We have to find ways to make our business operations more predictable and more systematized so that we can maintain some level of sanity when all of those external factors take us off course. We have to give our customers the impression that what is complex is simple, so that they can trust our actions.

I think back to the days when I began dental school. My parents didn't have the money to send me to school, but my focus to succeed was so great that I never feared the challenge of what lay ahead. I didn't fear failure, and I found ways to afford the mental and financial expenses that I had to pay. That isn't to say that those years were easy. I never thought I would get those school loans paid off. But I did. I often thought that if I had known before dental school the challenges and obstacles I would face, I might not have pursued going to dental school. Ignorance is bliss. The fact is that it would not have mattered. The fact is that I had a fearless clarity. Fearless focus prevailed as I had the proper respect for the job at hand and made preparations for it.

Lap 3 Lesson: *I still recall a classmate who after graduation from dental school opened his new office—new equipment, new office, and a new corvette in the parking lot! What was I doing wrong? I could barely afford gas for my car. He is no longer in business today. He had a fearless clarity, but his ambition was blind. Prepare with your dream but live in reality.*

But keep this in mind. My recommendation is to have a fearless clarity, not a blind focus! Expect the unexpected. Keep your eyes open to all possibilities and always consider a worst-case scenario. That is part of being prepared for any challenge. I have to live with the fact that driving at high speeds can have significant consequences. I have to be honest with myself. I have

> My recommendation is to have a fearless clarity, not a blind focus!

to know that every time I go out on track, I could be injured or even killed. I have to anticipate the unexpected. I have to study and practice

Have a fearless clarity
not a blind focus!

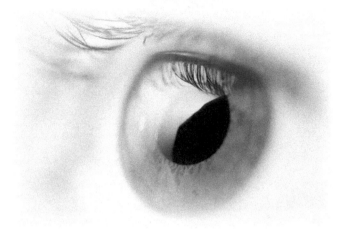

Expect the unexpected and
keep your eyes open
to all possibilities.

my craft to improve my odds. My wife also insists I have life insurance. Remember, there is a complexity to simplicity. It is our mission to complete our task and to make the completion process as predictable as possible. If we can make things more predictable, our task becomes easier. Go fast, my friend, and do it without fear, but respect the possibilities. Prepare in every way possible to succeed. Be fearless, not blind.

Lap 3 Tipping Point
Have a fearless clarity not a blind focus!
Expect the unexpected. Keep your
eyes open to all possibilities and always
consider a worst-case scenario.

Lap 4
Memories or Dreams?

~~~~~~

An interesting thing happened as soon as I got off the racetrack that morning. I had just had my best lap ever at Hallett, yet I immediately looked for ways to go even faster. I consulted with my crew. We looked at the car setup. We discussed tire pressures and engine performance, and we discussed driving techniques that could make me better. I downloaded information from the computer so that I could evaluate every component of the car while on track. I viewed the in-car video for ways to improve.

> Memories are a reflection of life. Dreams are a stimulus for life.

We constantly amend our strategy for the future. I constantly looked ahead to see how I could improve. Kirk Behrendt told me once, "When your memories are bigger than your dreams, you are stuck. Look ahead." That is a lesson that is said best in a song by the Dreamettes, "The strong keep getting stronger and move along. The weak keep getting weaker and they stay where they are." Look ahead. Here is what I believe: Memories are a reflection of life. Dreams are a stimulus for life.

Memories
are a reflection of life.

Dreams
are a stimulus for life.

This same lesson is important in our business too. When I go to consult with dentists and their teams, I have learned that many of the teams "get stuck." This has even been true in my own practice. My team has been an integral part of my practice for many years. The fact is that often things are done a particular way simply because "that is the way we have always done it." Kirk and I recently had this very discussion. No doubt it is difficult to teach an old dog new tricks. He told me something that is very powerful.

1. It is usually easier to kill a business than to significantly recreate it.

2. The hard part is not getting the new ideas IN. It is usually getting the old ideas OUT.

We have to constantly evolve and move ahead. Not that it is easy. Change is hard. But the adage that it is hard to teach an old dog new tricks has some level of truth. A perfect example is the use of technology in our practice. Many of my team members were technology challenged. So when we moved the direction of our practice to digital record keeping, there was resistance. It was not that they didn't want to use it; they didn't feel comfortable with its use. I had to say to them more than once, "Don't tell me the reasons you can't do something; tell me why you can." The argument wasn't that they objected to something new. It was that it was easier to do things the way we had always done them in the past. Interestingly, once they started to use the new technology, record keeping became easier, and they became comfortable using the computer and the system. What was once a challenge became routine and predictable. So what was the benefit? Our team is more efficient, our records are managed much better, and our patients constantly comment on how up-to-date we keep our practice.

> "Don't tell me the reasons you can't do something; tell me why you can."

Lap 4 Lesson: *It is amazing how the lines will form at the Apple store for the latest, greatest iPhone. It is a remarkable piece of equipment, no doubt. But the fact is that by time we purchase the latest-generation phone, the elves are back in the workshop looking for ways to make it even better. Always look ahead and be willing to recreate your success. Dreams stimulate life.*

You can take the idea of always looking forward even further. I had a patient who retired a few months ago. When he came in recently for an appointment, he told me that he might move. When I asked why, he said, "Because I am considering a new job." He explained that he had no direction, and he felt he had nothing to look forward to. If we don't look forward, we lose our stimulus to grow. You have heard so many stories of someone retiring, or of someone losing a long-time spouse, and in a short time they lose their desire for life. The point is that they have nothing to look forward to and that robs them of life. Reflect on the past, my friend, but live for today and dream for tomorrow.

> ## Lap 4 Tipping Point
> Memories are a reflection of life. Dreams are a stimulus for life. Look forward and constantly recreate your dreams.

Lap 5
Find Your Love

A study shows that kids of today's generation reach independence at a much older age than kids of my generation. In my day, independence was achieved at an average age of twenty-one. Research shows that today the average age is twenty-eight before independence is achieved. It is interesting, however, to note that those young adults who already have a vision of their future often reach independence sooner. In other words, developing clarity of vision is critical to success. It is for this reason that I expose my children to as many different possibilities and opportunities as possible. Since my son was ten years old he has raced cars. When he was fifteen years old, he started flying lessons.

This past summer I had him shadow three of my friends/patients who all operate or own various businesses. He has traveled with me to many of my speaking

> It is for this reason that I expose my children to as many different possibilities and opportunities as possible.

engagements and National Speakers Association conventions. My daughter has been heavily involved with horses, and she also spends time working at her barn. She works part-time in my office. She too has traveled to many of my seminars. Their exposure to different opportunities has led both of my kids to major in entrepreneurial business in college. I have purposefully given them different opportunities and exposed them to various events so they can develop their dream. I have exposed them to these various opportunities in an effort to find something that might connect with them at a deeper level. It is important that they should be given opportunities to develop their dreams through exposure to many possibilities.

> I have exposed them to these various opportunities in an effort to find something that might connect with them at a deeper level.

Kids learn from everything they do. If their explorations bring pleasure or success, they will want to learn more. Kids who receive support and encouragement are more likely to develop their own dreams sooner than those who don't. Kids who do not receive this support and interaction are likely to have a much different attitude about developing their dreams.

Often, people do things simply because they want to do them. This choice is the result of what I call "inside juices." People make their own choices and achieve satisfaction from both the act of choosing and from the result of that choice. My daughter loves to shop. She loves the fact that she gets to make her own choice, and she loves the new blouse that she gets to wear too. Since the activity generates the motivation, the process is mostly self-sustaining for as long as she wants to continue the activity—and as long as her parents pay for it!

Maybe this isn't the best example.

People also engage in activities in an effort to please someone else. These activities are a result of "outside juices." When someone is extrinsically motivated, the reward comes from outside; it has to be provided by someone else and has to be continually given to produce the motivation to continue the activity. As I think about it, my daughter's shopping may be more from "outside juices" when I pay for it. Maybe that is why it is more gratifying for her when she earns the money herself.

Find your love.

Inside-juice activity is more rewarding in and of itself. Intrinsically motivated people are more involved in their own growth and development. In other words, they are more likely to learn and create their dreams when they are intrinsically motivated, and thus the importance of exposing people to different opportunities that might create meaningful connection. This is why it is more important that my kids' dreams are their own dreams and not what I may impose on them. How many times have you seen parents try to impose their will on a child and fail miserably?

Lap 5 Lesson: *How many times have you seen parents who get angry with their child because they are living through their child's experience? I coached my daughter's softball team for years. We often commented that it was easier to coach the children than it was the parents. We often forget that our dreams may not be our children's dreams too. Allow your children the opportunity to follow what drives them...not what drives you the parent. No doubt this is a tough lesson, even for me!*

There are a number of behavioral characteristics we can consider for ourselves, for our children, and for our team. These are indicators of high motivation.

Persistence: A highly motivated person will stay involved for a long period of time, whereas an unmotivated person will give up very easily when not instantly successful. People learn persistence when they are successful at a challenging task. The art of building persistence is in offering a task that is just challenging enough, but not overwhelming.

Choice of challenge is another characteristic of motivation. People who are challenged and succeed become motivated. Motivated learners will choose an activity that is slightly difficult for them, but provides an appropriate challenge. People who are unmotivated will pick something that is very easy and ensures instant success. They have a low level of satisfaction because they know that the task offers little challenge.

Independence is an important aspect of quality growth and learning. People with strong inside juices do not need constant oversight. People who have a lower level of motivation or are motivated by outside juices need constant attention and have more difficulty functioning independently.

Spirit is also an indicator of motivation. People who are clearly motivated will display spirit. People without appropriate motivation will not take any apparent pleasure in their activity and will often complain.

You can begin to see the importance of an internal reward system and that it can be more meaningful than an external system. In an outside-juice model, people can begin to feel successful only if *someone else* rewards them for their accomplishments. They lose their inside juices and may only feel successful when someone else judges them to be successful. This can have a great effect on self-esteem.

We can apply that lesson to our businesses too. When our teams are constantly exposed to new or different things, they expand and connect with things that have meaning for them. In turn, that can be the connection that stimulates them to improve and grow. I have found that when people find a meaningful

> **If you work at something you love, it doesn't seem like work.**

connection, that connection gets the inside juices going. Those juices flow best when the connection is to something they love. You have heard it before. If you work at something you love, it doesn't seem like work. Work is work, but if you are challenged by something that is fulfilling and churns the inside juices, work is more enjoyable.

Lap 5 Tipping Point
Expose yourself and those around you to opportunities so a connection can be made that inspires growth with something you love.

Lap 6

We Love to Fly
and It Shows

You can really tell when somebody loves what he or she does. I am reminded of this often when I travel. I fly a lot. Years ago I started building miles with American Airlines. Almost five million miles later—Platinum for life! I will fly other carriers if I can get a direct flight. I have noticed a few interesting things on my journeys. Here are some of the opinions that I have developed in my years of traveling:

1. On most carriers the employees are not thrilled with their company and there is a very high level of frustration in the industry. Of course there are always exceptions.

2. In general, I find a much better disposition with crews/employees who fly for Southwest Airlines. They seem to enjoy what they do more and they consistently praise their company. Their announcements are much funnier too.

3. If you want to be on time, your best bet is Southwest Airlines.

4. The magazines in the seat pockets on all carriers are the same except that each magazine has a different CEO

explaining why their airline is so great. They all emphasize that their airline values each one of us.

5. People don't even get upset anymore if a flight is late or cancelled because this has become so common.

6. Even though you may pay extra to have your luggage travel with you, it can still be lost.

7. Most airline employees you talk to in the industry will tell you that the best company to work for is Southwest Airlines.

As I make these observations, please understand that this is not a scientific finding. It is only what I have observed and perceived. Also note that I have no special interest at all in Southwest Airlines. That being said, consider this:

I recently took a flight from Oklahoma City to Miami on American Airlines. Sitting next to me was a flight attendant for American Airlines. She was heading back home after completing her annual training. She had been with the company for almost thirty years. It was obvious to me that she was a genuine and caring person. Yet she told me that she was simply putting in her time and in six years she would retire. She was very angry with her company. Why? They had just completed negotiations for restructuring while the company was in bankruptcy. Her expectations and reality didn't match. Her opinion was that the bankruptcy was a ploy for reorganization even though they had $5.5 billion dollars in the bank. She never expected to have to take a pay decrease and have her retirement affected after all the years she had served with the company.

I don't know if the facts that she gave me were correct or not. I do know that was her perception of the facts. I do know she was upset at the reduction in pay and benefits regardless of whether the bankruptcy was genuine or not. So I did some investigative research. The flight attendant explained to me that American Airlines attendants would now earn wages and benefits similar to those of Southwest Airlines flight attendants. After restructuring, she said, on average, American Airlines pilots would still earn as much or more money than Southwest Airlines pilots.

Now think about this. According to the flight attendant, even after restructuring, the pay earned by American Airlines employees was similar to or higher than their competitor. So why does one group of employees—those who work for Southwest Airlines—appear to be fulfilled and happy while the other group of employees from American Airlines seem to be angry and unhappy? Here is the important difference: it is related to their culture. From their very first contact with the company, people employed by Southwest Airlines feel that the company really cares about them. The flight attendant who had just returned from her training didn't feel her company really cared about her at all.

Here is something to consider. In our business, our primary concern is not just to take care of our clients. Rather, we should take care of our team, and in turn, they will take care of our clients. Now that is not to say that a team will get everything it desires. We cannot give benefits beyond reason or to a point that isn't viable for the success of our business. Remember

> We should take care of our team, and in turn, they will take care of our clients.

what I said. It can't have a blind focus. But the fact is that if we concentrate on the care and well-being of our team, they, in turn, will take care of us. That is a cultural shift.

In my opinion, here is what has happened in the airline industry. The entire culture of "how" is a disaster. How customers are ticketed, the inflexibility of the system, and the lack of relationship with the customer and their employees are fatal. Unfortunately, the system takes precedent over the relationship. Many employees in the industry don't feel the love either. Did the results cited by the American Consumer Satisfaction Index happen by chance? The survey, which ranked customer satisfaction in service industries on a scale of 0–100, found that airline passenger satisfaction dropped by 1.5 percent to a score of sixty-five. This score ties the airline industry to the newspaper industry as the most disappointing sectors ACSI rates. Baggage fees are to blame, according to the survey. Those who shell out for their luggage charted a satisfaction score of fifty-eight compared to sixty-eight for those flying fee free.

The disgruntled public comes from "Customers experiencing overall costs going up, but the experience is not getting better." At the head of the pack, Southwest Airlines (with no fees for the first two checked bags) has held top ranking for the past eighteen years. It is not just the fact that passengers' bags fly for free that sets this airline apart. It is because the company has set up a culture that reflects care for its employees. It turn, happy employees take care of the company.

> **It is because the company has set up a culture that reflects care for its employees.**

The fact is that the airline industry is a big machine that will be very difficult to change. The culture of the industry is not personal. There is little flexibility in the system. This is the reason that many customers have become silently enraged with cramped seats, delays, and cancelled flights. As customers of the industry, we know we cannot change the system, and we too feel as if the culture doesn't care.

Lap 6 Lesson: *I recently took a business flight. There were two lines of people waiting to be seen at the ticket counter, I stood in line, waiting my turn. For some reason, our line was being overlooked. When another passenger asked the agent if he could serve our line too, the agent replied, "You will need to talk to the supervisor." He didn't have the authority to take care of a customer's complaint. Not only was the customer ignored, but the other people in line became irritated too. The agent worked in a culture that didn't allow him to be his best. Join a culture that allows you to be your best and everyone will benefit.*

According to the Bureau of Transportation statistics, 76 percent of flights are on time. That means one out of four flights will not be on time. There can still be wonderful people who are helpful and caring, but they work in a culture that seems helpless. So when we can fly on a carrier that is on time with a team that seems fulfilled and happy, we love it. The point is that our culture means everything. While systems matter, the culture in which they exist is the primary foundation. It is

> It is very difficult to change a culture. That is why you should exercise caution before joining a team whose culture you don't understand.

very difficult to change a culture. That is why you should exercise caution before joining a team whose culture you don't understand.

It is hard to change a culture,

so keep that in mind before you choose to join one.

The American Airlines flight attendant felt the company didn't care about her. As a matter of fact she said, "I don't think the culture of our company even allows them to tell us thank you or that they appreciate us. I just want them to tell me thank you and that I matter." That is powerful.

The fact is the employees of American Airlines are typically very personable and caring people. And I am sure that if you could spend time with the executives of the company, you would find they really do care too. What screams "I don't care" is the culture in which they have to work. It limits their effectiveness. Their culture has allowed systems to develop that are not employee- or customer-friendly. The key to the airline's success will not be a new slogan or a new magazine in the seat pocket. Rather, it will be the creation of a culture that expresses appreciation for employees and customers, not just with words but actions too.

Lap 6 Tipping Point
Understand a culture before you elect to join it. Create a culture that allows for appreciation of the team and the customers.

Lap 7

The Good, the Bad, and the Ugly

When a positive culture exists, great people using effective systems add to a positive predictability. When a negative culture exists, systems can add to a negative predictability. That is exactly the reason a pilot uses a checklist. Systems really do matter. I hate it when a pilot forgets to lower the landing gear before landing the plane. It makes such a mess and it is very noisy too. So you won't think I am picking on American Airlines, let me share an experience I had with their competitor, United Airlines.

> When a positive culture exists, great people using effective systems add to a positive predictability. When a negative culture exists, systems can add to a negative predictability.

I was traveling back to Oklahoma City after a day of consulting in a dental practice in North Carolina. I had a lay-over in Washington, DC. Our flight from North Carolina was forty-five minutes late, but no worries, because, during my lay-over in DC, I was to remain on the same plane, which then traveled to Oklahoma City. However, when we landed in DC, we all were asked to deplane.

Lap 7 Lesson: *Do systems really matter? A friend of mine purchased a new twin-engine airplane. On his first day of ownership, he flew with an instructor to receive the necessary training so he could be qualified to fly that particular aircraft. As they practiced single-engine approaches, a warning horn would sound, telling them that power was low on one engine and that the landing gear was not down. They had the power reduced on one engine to simulate conditions when that engine was not working properly. To eliminate the noise, the instructor pulled the circuit breaker that sounded the warning horn that indicated the gear was not down. After their practice, they returned to the airport to land. They made the final approach, but they had forgotten to lower the landing gear. Because the circuit breaker that warned of this problem had been pulled, they had no idea what was about to happen. On the first day he became the owner of his new airplane, my friend turned it into a boat—a perfect belly landing. The checklist wasn't followed and the lack of a system resulted in a negative predictability. Great systems increase positive predictability.*

As I left the plane, I came up to a gentleman standing at the end of the jet bridge. He asked if I was Dr. Fling? I replied, "Yes." He said, "I already have your boarding pass for the next flight to Oklahoma City, and I have a reservation for you at a nearby hotel." I was confused. I had to be home that night. I had patients confirmed for the entire next day. I told him I needed to get home that evening and I was supposed to be on the plane I had just left. He explained that the plane had been rerouted and there were no other flights available that would get me home that night. I wasn't happy, but I knew I couldn't fight the system.

The gentleman who helped me was very nice. He looked for other carriers and he searched for other possibilities. It wasn't his lack of care or concern that angered me. It was the culture and framework that he had to work within that angered me. While the CEO in the magazine said the airline cared about me, the fact that the flight had been rerouted told me something very different. The result for me, the customer, was ugly.

Systems matter.

So off to the hotel I went. I hadn't prepared for this delay; I didn't have clean socks or clean undies, and five hours of work the next day would be missed. There was no explanation from United as to why my plane had been rerouted, causing inconvenience to my patients and myself. Most of the people who work for both American and United really do care. However, the culture of their business models produces a system that results in customer dissatisfaction. When a negative culture exists, it can lead to a negative predictability.

So I wanted to express my dissatisfaction. I called the airline agent and she passed me along to customer service (after a lengthy hold and a twenty-two-step, automated process before human assistance could be reached). I explained my dissatisfaction. Here is the company's system for handling my complaint: the customer service department didn't take complaints! I thought it was odd that the customer service department couldn't provide service for the customer. Instead, I would have to submit my complaint by e-mail. It would be reviewed and someone would contact me later. Now that is customer service! Once again, I believe people are the strong points. They really do care. They don't want me to be late any more than I do. The culture and the systems the industry has in place simply don't allow employees to be their best. So once again, choose your culture carefully and know that systems can bring either good or bad results. The bottom line is to create systems that are founded with a positive culture that creates a great experience for the customer.

Lap 7 Tipping Point
Systems can bring good or bad results.
Utilize systems within a positive culture
that result in great experiences.

Lap 8
A Great Latte

I love the culture and my experience and when I go to Starbucks. I find the experience as good as the coffee. Venti, nonfat, no-foam, no-water, seven-pump chai is my favorite. That is a mouthful, isn't it? You recall I have mentioned my colleague Kirk Behrendt. He has been such a game changer for me. He owns a company called ACT Dental that coaches dental teams all around the country. Years ago he heard of my dental practice. He came to visit and observe me and my team in action. He was looking for model practices that could serve as an example for his clients. He was looking for ways to help his clients develop their clarity by allowing them to observe us in action.

When we went to dinner, after he had spent the day in my practice, he commented, "You are like the Starbucks of dental practices." I asked him to explain. He commented that through-out the day he had seen patients who had had a calm and pleasant experience. He also commented on how systematized every aspect of our practice seemed. From how we answered the phone, set up our treatment rooms or how the bathrooms were cleaned, there was a remarkable consistency and feeling about our practice.

It was a great experience for the team and our customers. It reminded him of his favorite place too—Starbucks. He then conveyed something to me that has remarkable meaning: "People don't run your business. Systems do. And people run the systems." I had never given that much thought to the way my practice worked. But as I contemplated what he had said, I agreed. Don't misunderstand. You still have to have great people to run the system. But it is the system that will navigate your business, just as at Starbucks, which operates a predictable system that allows over 83,000 different drink combinations to be made with predictable consistency. It isn't that Starbucks hires the best latte makers. The company has a great system with great people who operate those systems to give their customers consistency and a great experience.

> "People don't run your business. Systems do. And people run the systems."

Lap 8 Lesson: *I love sitting in the leather chair in the corner of the store at my local Starbucks. It isn't just the coffee. It is the experience. The founder of Starbucks said, "We are not in the coffee business serving people. We are in the people business serving coffee". Have great people utilize great systems to create predictability and an exceptional experience.*

And here is the reason these systems became so critical. Great systems allow people to perform a task efficiently and predictably. Once that occurs, you have more time to spend on the thing that makes such a difference with your clients: the relationship and the experience. Think about it. At Starbucks I get my favorite drink

"Systems run
the business
and people run
the systems."
Kirk Behrendt

made right, almost every time, in a place that has a caring culture and gives me a great feeling. It is great people, using a great system that is reinforced by a caring culture. With a combination like that, I don't mind paying $5 for a cup of coffee. That is a great latte!

Lap 8 Tipping Point
Great people using great systems in a caring culture combine for a great result.

Lap 9
Hang Ten

A number of years ago my family took our first trip to Hawaii. While on Maui, the ocean called us all to take surf lessons. In Oklahoma, we don't have a lot of great surfing. So this was going to be a challenge. We took our boards out into the water and tried to "hang ten." Needless to say, we didn't hang anything except our egos.

Soon, the instructor called us into the shore as he reviewed the fundamentals of successfully standing on a board while in motion on the water. To my best recollection, the trick was to keep your hands on the board, bringing one knee in front of the other between your arms, raising your posterior section up, and then letting your hands go in order to stand upright. The trick was to not let your hands go before you raised your posterior section. This sequence of events just didn't seem natural. But with great instruction and by practicing an unnatural sequence until it seemed natural, we continued to practice that sequence over and over and over.

Then we took our new system into the water. We followed the steps we had practiced on the beach, and before long it was like magic: we were surfing. Now you can guess who was the most proficient surfer—my young daughter, Kinsey. But let me tell you just what a great student I was. We actually took surf school a second day too. I looked for ways to get better. I challenged myself to improve. Much as in the race car, I was already looking for ways to improve and raise the bar. I practiced the system my instructor had given me over and over. I feared nothing. And by the time we were finished, I became such a natural that I actually surfed waves that were over twelve . . . inches tall!

Lap 9 Lesson: *My favorite track that I raced in my formula car was Texas Motor Speedway. One year I actually won the race, even competing against a professional team. I still remember the thrill of victory. As we entered turns one and two, the track was set up as a road course. They had us go low on the apron in an effort to slow us down. They wanted to reduce the speeds of the cars, as we had to brake hard down a long backstretch so we could enter some turns on the infield. The really fast guys took turns one and two flat out. It was unnerving at first. You felt that the car would not hold its rear grip through the turns and that it would spin out. But keeping the gas on and not letting up was necessary if you wanted to run up-front. So, I had to take a risk. And I did. I learned the importance of calculated risk and to trust the choice I made. It didn't feel comfortable at first. But soon I was fast too.*

It took a good teacher, with a great system, and it required that I be willing to take a risk. It took a good teacher, with a great system, and it required that I be willing to take a risk. I had to trust my instructor and then perform. It is no different with our team.

It took a
good teacher,
with a
great system,
and it required that I be
willing to
take a risk.

We have to have a great leader, use great systems, and be willing to risk. Some have the talent to surf the large waves, and others, the small ones. The point is that great systems first have to be developed, and then time has to be allowed to practice. Having great systems and a willingness to risk while applying your knowledge can yield great results so that you can hang ten too.

Lap 9 Tipping Point
Risk and practice an unnatural
system until it becomes natural.

Lap 10
The Big Yellow Bus

Before I had documented and refined my business systems to the degree at which they are today, I had an experience that illustrates the importance of great systems. My team is comprised of one front-office person (Tammy) and one team member who works both in the front office and in the clinical area (Bonnie). I have an assistant (Crystal) who works entirely in the clinical area along with my two hygienists (Beverly and Janie). Tammy was going to be gone on a family vacation for two weeks to Hawaii. I wasn't invited, so I stayed back to hold the fort down. Our solution to Tammy's being gone for two weeks was to keep Bonnie up front, Crystal in the back, and allow the hygienists to carry on in their usual clinical areas.

It was the second workday of Tammy's two-week absence when, early that morning, I looked through the doorway of my treatment room to see Bonnie standing in the hallway. I could tell by the look on her face that something wasn't right. A tear came down from her eye. I asked, "What was wrong?" She said, "I have to go to the hospital right now!"

Bonnie had to have surgery that day, and thank goodness she had a great recovery. I still am not sure how, but somehow we made in through the day. Missing two vital team members, we were exhausted at day's end. Crystal and I celebrated our survival without the other two team members. It was time to call it a day. I asked Crystal to set the phone recording so we could go home. Guess what? We didn't know how! You see, Tammy was running the front office, not the system. When Tammy wasn't present we were lost.

This is what can happen when people run your business and not the systems. No doubt Tammy is amazing. But if we had an appropriate system in place, we would have known how to navigate through adversity even when Tammy wasn't present. We would have known how to activate the recorder even when she was gone.

It was after that episode I insisted that we develop, document, and utilize a system for everything we did in our business. From how we activated the answering service to clinical procedures, to cleaning the bathrooms. A documented system was completed and put into writing. Then the team members reviewed those systems so that they had a complete understanding of the tasks at hand.

Lap 10 Lesson: *Talented people may never have the opportunity to excel if they are not part of a great system. Think of all the extraordinarily talented athletes who never reached the pinnacle of their sport because they didn't have a system to support their talent. I think of possibly the greatest running back of all time, Barry Sanders. Was it that he didn't have the other talent to support him, or that the systems didn't support the team? Great systems allow great talent to predictably soar.*

Today we have a saying that is a little twisted, but it expresses the importance of our systems. We joke that, "We want our systems documented and followed so well, that if a big yellow bus hits Tammy, another team member can step in and fulfill the task at hand." I don't want to diminish the value of Tammy and the rest of my team. They are all amazing and exceptional. But if Tammy is aware that Ms. Smith doesn't want us to call her before 10 AM and that Ms. Smith has a financial arrangement to pay $100/month, I don't want that information logged only inside Tammy's head. If that big yellow bus does hit Tammy and we don't have the system to know those details, we waste time and energy, not to mention upsetting our customers.

So we have a system that documents special notes for our clients and we have a system that defines financial arrangements and expectations. It is a system that can be accessed by any member of the team. These systems allow Tammy to be more efficient so that she has time to be the remarkable person that she is. Now she is free to develop and nurture the most important component of our work with our clients: the relationship and their experience. Because every system is documented and the team is cross-trained, another team member can step in and operate that system when she is absent.

I make sure Tammy looks both ways before she crosses the street. And she has to totally avoid school zones! But she too understands the importance of great systems.

Lap 10 Tipping Point
Insist on developing, documenting,
and using a system for everything
you do in your business.

Lap 11

Don't Be Fooled

D an was a single guy living at home with his father and he worked in the family business. When he found out he was going to inherit a fortune after his sick father died, he decided he needed to find a wife with whom to share his fortune. One evening, at an investment meeting, he spotted the most beautiful woman he had ever seen. Her natural beauty took his breath away. "I may look like just an ordinary guy," he said to her, "but in just a few years, my father will die and I will inherit over $200 million." Impressed, the woman asked for his business card and three weeks later, she became his stepmother. **Sometimes we just "think" we know and we make poor assumptions.**

We think we know what we know, but often we don't know we don't know. I'm so confused. After our incident with Bonnie's surgery, we worked hard to develop and document our systems. We thought we were on our way. Tammy had written the system on how to activate the recorder, and I had the system documented on how to make the coffee. What else did we need? Crystal followed the directions that Tammy had documented, and guess what? It was really bad coffee. We were fooled. We thought the system and instruction we had developed was complete, but instead we found that we took some things for granted.

> We think we know what we know, but often we don't know we don't know.

Lap 11 Lesson: *There is a great adage to learning. The curve to learning starts with "You don't know you don't know." Then as you learn, you become aware that "you know you don't know." Then you progress until "you know you know," and finally mastery occurs when "you don't know you know." Evaluate where you are and don't make assumptions.*

Don't assume. Verify.

Much like Dan we made some assumptions that gave us unpredictable results. When Tammy wrote our new system, she assumed that Crystal understood some of the minor details that were pertinent to the system to be successful. In reality she didn't understand many of the details that Tammy had taken for granted. So we had to rewrite those systems. We had to do it in a way that allowed someone who wasn't familiar with that task to complete it successfully. We had to document it so well that even I could do it! That is a critical part to completing systems. The most successful teams are the teams that are highly detailed and highly cross-trained. Documentation has to be so complete that team members who are ignorant of that process can find their way through it. Like riding that wave, you get better with practice and doing.

Much like our dreams, our systems often need to be amended and updated. Don't be fooled and assume. Verify.

Lap 11 Tipping Point

The most successful teams are those that are highly detailed and highly cross-trained.

Document systems so completely that someone who isn't familiar with a task can complete it successfully.

Lap 12
The Fabric of Who We Are

*I*f systems run the practice, do people matter? Of course they do! It takes the right people to run the systems. In my profession, the average turnover rate for an employee is less than two years. Somehow, I have managed to retain my staff much longer: Tammy, twenty-two years; Bonnie, twelve years; Crystal, six years; and my hygienists (Beverly and Janie), each more than thirty-six years! I purchased my practice from Dr. Bill Lockard. Those hygienists worked for him, and they have continued to work with me. So what is the key to having such a stable team that runs the office like a Starbucks? There are a number of key factors.

First, they are simply great people. By that I mean that their values and character are remarkable. They want to care, they like to smile, and they value what they provide for our clients. Many of my staff were hired with no dental experience at all. To have a great person is more

> To have a great person is more valuable than having a well-trained person with poor character and values.

Having a great person is more valuable than having a well-trained person with poor character and values.

valuable than having a well-trained person with poor character and values. We teach our team our culture; they learn our systems, but it is being caring, responsible people that sets them apart. My team knows my passion for and commitment to quality in everything we do. They relate to the quality and culture that I demand. I make them aware of my vision. I believe it is providing a clear purpose and philosophy and having clarity about expectations that holds them to a standard that is fulfilling for us all. I also understand that great people often work in a setting where things just don't work out for one or both parties. It takes mutual appreciation for the philosophy to work between the business model and the people who deliver that model. It starts with having great clarity and then measuring for success.

> It takes mutual appreciation for the philosophy to work between the business model and the people who deliver that model.

Lap 12 Lesson: *Far too often we get caught up in great grades or ways to measure success. Success is often measured on completion of tasks or how you compare to others. My son, Tyler, has a learning difference that makes school very hard. He makes it, but at the Fling house, we celebrate Cs. I never thought I would be okay with that, but I am. You know what? He works his tail off and he is a great person. That is a bigger measure of success than a great grade.*

Lap 12 Tipping Point

Having a great staff member is more valuable than having a well-trained staff member with poor character and values. Mutual appreciation for the philosophy between the business model and the people who deliver that model must be developed.

Lap 13
Resolving Conflict

inety percent of all associateships/partnerships in dentistry fail. The biggest reason these are not successful isn't because the partners are bad people. It is because there is a difference in the partners' philosophies. When what you get is different from what you think you are going to get, conflict arises.

People enter a partnership with certain expectations. When they find a difference between the reality and their expectations, conflict enters.

> When what you get is different from what you think you are going to get, conflict arises.

I have often heard leaders of a business concern themselves with the need to terminate someone's employment because that person is not fulfilling his or her responsibilities or he or she doesn't fit within the culture that exists. But often these leaders rationalize that they cannot afford to "let them go." My contention is that you can't afford to keep such employees.

Find great people who reflect your philosophy who are committed, who can share your vision and develop systems they can use. Then they will serve you well. When you are looking to

When what you get is different from what you think you are going to get... ...conflict arises.

find someone to join your team, look beyond simply what they can do. Instead, confirm mutual philosophies and then be clear about expectations.

Lap 13 Lesson: *I had a patient I inherited from another practice. He didn't know me at all. As I got to know his mouth, I saw obvious problems. He questioned my diagnosis and my request that he should have X-rays. He thought I was just making stuff up. As we talked, he told me he liked my hygienist Janie, but he didn't like me. He said he would like to continue to see her, but he just didn't want to see me. I explained to him that I didn't see how he could come to that conclusion when he didn't even know me. I also explained that Janie and I were a team and that he couldn't have one without the other. I suggested that it would be best for him to find a new dentist, as I wasn't feeling the love either. A few months later he was on the schedule again. He agreed to let us gather the needed diagnostic information I had suggested. He reluctantly trusted me. I found the decay that I had suspected. I asked him to return to have some fillings. I decided to place the necessary fillings at no charge. I wanted to prove a point to him; I wanted him to know it wasn't about the money; it was about doing the right thing for him. I finally gained his trust and I think he may actually like me now. The level of care that we provided was just different from what he had received in the past. What he got was different from what he thought he was going to get. I had to bring trust to that process.*

I recently conducted an all-day class with some teams in Fresno, California. There was a man in the audience named Bill Clark who shared with me an adage that he had conveyed to his children as they were growing up. He said, "It's what you do that you don't have to do that will always determine what you are, when it is too late to do anything about it." That is profound. I believe that summarizes what makes a team member exceptional. It is the little things that go beyond what is expected that can make the difference: sending a hand-written note to patients, telling patients how grateful you are to have them in your practice, sending a birthday card, or sincerely asking patients how they are. It is the phone call during after-hours, or a touch on the arm, that can make the difference.

> "It's what you do that you don't have to do that will always determine what you are, when it is too late to do anything about it."

It is indeed the little things that can make a big difference. It is those little things that will make you who you are. And remember, now is the time. In other words, don't look back to find out the opportunity to make a difference has passed you by.

Finding team members who subscribe to the same philosophy is the first step in reducing conflict that may arise from unfilled expectations.

Lap 13 Tipping Point
Reduce conflict by developing a team that is bound by a congruent philosophy and clear expectations.

Lap 14
Fake It

The truth is that every day can't be a great day. There can always be a circumstance that causes you to feel less than your best. So what does my team do when our tank isn't running on full? **We fake it!** (Meg Ryan doesn't have a corner on the market.) It is amazing what happens those days when we have to fake it. We find that by day's end we somehow feel better. Take care

> Take care of your team, your family, and even yourself during times when you're down.

of your team, your family, and even yourself during times when you're down. Fake it and you will be surprised just how it will improve your world.

So what does my team do when our **tank isn't running on full?**

Lap 14 Lesson: *Meg Ryan hasn't cornered the market on faking it. Let me explain. Like everyone else, I sometimes feel "down" too. I was having one of those episodes a few weeks ago regarding a class I was teaching. While I was visiting with one of my colleagues about how I was down about the class, he said, "Mike, I wish you could sometimes see yourself the way that others perceive you." In other words, even though I may not always feel the strongest inside, others may perceive me in a positive way. His point? Improve my attitude by faking it even when I am "down." The result is a happier me.*

Lap 15
A Five-Letter Word

My daughter, Kinsey, is a wonderful young lady and an excellent equestrian. She works hard at her craft. One of her champion horses, Cowboy, has always placed well when she is in the saddle. The control she has with this large animal with the just the subtlest of inputs is amazing. It is her talent in conjunction with continued training and constant repetition that contribute to her success. There are times Kinsey would rather be socializing with friends or resting at home instead of working with her horse. But much like working with our team, it takes talent, praise, and constant repetition to achieve her goals.

Early one year (after a great season the year before with her horse), Kinsey had a horse show. As Cowboy entered the arena, he freaked out and was almost uncontrollable. At the next show he frantically ran around the arena, apparently trying to throw his mount. We were puzzled. Either Kinsey had lost her touch or our champion horse was going crazy. As it turns out, we learned there was a bigger issue. Cowboy was going blind in one eye. A new arena, seeing a new fence, even a new colored background, would spook his spirit.

Lap 15 Lesson: *As a dentist, I have many new patients who come into the office with high levels of fear. Going to the dentist isn't always a lot of fun. I have learned that my patients' fear is often not related to pain. Once I can demonstrate my touch, compassion, and care, their fears are reduced or eliminated. Why? Because they have learned to trust me. Providing consistent care, skill, and judgment helps build a trusting relationship.*

My wife and daughter were devastated. He became spooked at the slightest of unknowns. This horse was family. Let me put this in perspective. There is a pecking order in our family. It goes like this. Wife, children, horses/dog (they are a tie), me. So now what? We didn't know what to do.

> **His behavior was based upon his fear.**

Our trainer was pessimistic and suggested that Cowboy might need to be put out to pasture. There were tears at our house. By chance we met a trainer who said that all might not be lost. She suggested that his behavior was based upon his fear. Because his sight was impaired, he didn't trust his surroundings anymore. We learned that often you could work with a horse so that he learns to trust you and trust himself, and he could regain his champion composure and form. So the work began. Kinsey has worked hard with Cowboy. She has nurtured, delivered consistency, and become one with him in such a way that he once again can trust her and trust himself. Today, he is

> **Kinsey has provided the leadership, and Cowboy now trusts her input even with limited sight.**

Developing trust is
fundamental
to change.

back to his championship form. Kinsey has provided the leadership, and Cowboy now trusts her input even with limited sight.

Our team is no different. Once team members trust our input and leadership, they learn to take a risk and they acquire the potential to be a great team member. Even when someone's sight is impaired, developing trust contributes to creating championship form. Trust is not just a five-letter word.

Lap 15 Tipping Point
Developing trust is fundamental to change.

Lap 16

Work Is a Four-Letter Word

used to think that my goal was to achieve a balance in life. Consider a time in your life or in your business when there were events or circumstances that put your life or business out of balance. I can still recall the early days of my practice when things were tough. School loans, business debt, and worries of survival were constant. I worked 8 AM to 8 PM and was on call every weekend, so life was not in balance.

If you will honestly reflect about those days that were out of balance, you will find that it is at those times that growth often occurs. Those are times when you achieve incredible fulfillment. It is facing those challenges when your life is out of balance that yields amazing opportunity. No doubt living a life that has extreme imbalance isn't healthy.

But, with reasonable challenges, being out of balance can lead to significant change and growth. No doubt my focus on swimming thirty-two laps put my body and mind out of balance, but as I worked up to that distance, what was difficult became my norm. Awesome!

Lap 16 Lesson: *What gets monitored, gets improved. That is a fact of business. When we started a new system for tracking certain statistics of our performance, we learned that some areas of my business could be improved. It was becoming aware of our deficiencies that challenged us and stimulated our growth. I don't want to suggest that it is always easy. But it was this awareness that stimulated us to grow. If we had never been set off balance with these challenges, we might not have had the motivation to grow and improve.*

My team will tell you that work is a "four-letter word." Said another way, work isn't always easy. It is when we have those times of challenge,

> My team will tell you that work is a "four-letter word."

adversity, or change that leads us to growth opportunities. It is in those times of unbalance that we expand our comfort level and have the opportunity for growth. I am not suggesting that meeting these challenges is easy. Work is work. Look at every opportunity that disrupts your balance as a time for growth. This may sound a little silly, but even so, when things become routine and we lack the stimulus to grow, we lose the stimulus to grow. It sounds funny doesn't it? The point is to embrace challenge and reasonable unbalance in a healthy way, and you will find opportunity for growth.

Lap 16 Tipping Point
Embrace challenge and a reasonable unbalance to find an opportunity for growth.

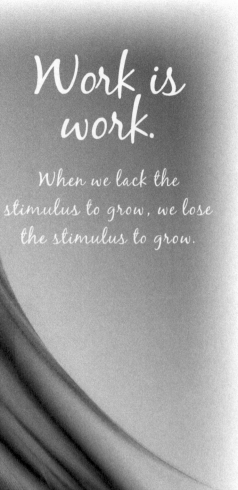

Work is work.

When we lack the stimulus to grow, we lose the stimulus to grow.

Lap 17
You Are Fired!

eff has been my best friend since second grade. We grew up together, went to school together, and trained as lab technicians together. He started his own business as a lab technician many years ago and I went on to dental school. Over the years we have laughed, cried, dreamed, and consoled each other. It has been said that in a lifetime you only have a few really close friends. Jeff is one of those friends.

Jeff knows that when I was in dental school, I had a vision that I was going to be a remarkable, restorative dentist. For whatever reason, I had a drive and passion to be the best dentist there was. In retrospect, that is ridiculous. Instead, I should have dreamed to be the best I could be. While maturity does bring gray hair, less hair, and a few muscle aches, it has its advantages in that it also brings a little wisdom. So I grew a start-up dental practice with a vision to be the best. I thought I knew all the things that had to be done to excel. After five years in practice, with Jeff working as my lab technician, I received a call from him one day.

He said, "Mike, you are going to have to find a new lab."

I was dumbfounded. I asked, "Why? Are you going to do something else?"

He said, "No, I'm not going to do anything else, but I can't keep doing this for you. You are going to have to find another lab because your stuff is horrible. You expect great things from me, but you don't provide me with what I need to give you the best."

I was getting fired! My thoughts were that he couldn't fire me. He must have forgotten that I was going to be the best. While we shared a common vision for remarkable outcomes, I didn't have the pieces in place to provide what was needed for him or me to be at our best.

> ## I simply didn't have the systems, a culture or a clear vision in place of *how* to achieve the desired results.

There was a difference between expectations and reality and that created conflict. So much so that Jeff was ready to send me on my way. We had the same philosophical approach in that we wanted to provide remarkable results. I simply didn't have the systems, a culture or a clear vision in place of *how* to achieve the desired results.

In dental school and when starting my practice in Oklahoma City, I would hear about this remarkable dentist named Dr. Bill Lockard. He was a teacher, a practitioner, and a mentor to many. In dental circles, he was a who's who of dentists. As it so happened, he was considering retirement at the time I was looking to expand my practice. This was during the same period when Jeff was frustrated with me. I investigated the possibility of purchasing Dr. Lockard's practice. After thoughtful deliberation, Dr. Lockard and I struck a deal. My theory was if you can't beat 'em, buy 'em. Jeff will attest to the fact that it was as though, overnight, my practice was transformed. The outcomes and the quality of all that I provided Jeff changed completely. I now provided Jeff with the necessities so that we could both be at our best. The outcomes Jeff and I produced together as a team improved exponentially.

Lap 17 Lesson: *Mentorships matter. Just think of the role that fathers play in the lives of their children. When kids don't have that mentorship, they suffer from a higher level of failure in school, poorer health, well-being, and overall success. Dr. Lockard was like a father to me in dentistry. Finding a mentor in business is essential.*

I even matured to the point where I learned it was more important for me to be the best *I* could be rather than being the best. So what made the difference? It was Dr. Lockard's mentorship and remarkable systems that truly transformed my life. He had established a remarkable culture that was reinforced with great systems that I was able to utilize.

I was a very visual learner. I could watch how he did things. He had all of the systems in place with his team and they were empowered to produce exceptional outcomes. He nurtured, he inspired, he demanded, he demonstrated, and he held me to a higher standard. He made me accountable. It was having a fearless clarity and like-minded philosophies that allowed the application of his systems through his mentorship to help me to grow my potential.

> It was Dr. Lockard's mentorship and remarkable systems that truly transformed my life. He had established a remarkable culture that was reinforced with great systems that I was able to utilize.

Surround yourself with great people...

...and learn from them and their culture.

The point is that great systems and mentorship from a master really make a difference. You will find that in almost any business or industry, and in our personal lives too, there

> Surround yourself with great people and learn from them and their culture.

are mentors we turn to who can give us remarkable direction. Often, you just have to ask. Surround yourself with great people and learn from them and their culture.

Lap 17 Tipping Point
Become the best you can be with the guidance of great mentors.

Lap 18
Give and Receive

When I inherited the culture that Dr. Lockard had developed, I pulled what I call a "Barry Switzer." Remember, I am from Oklahoma, and I am an Oklahoma University graduate. In our neck of the woods, coach Switzer is godlike. After he left Oklahoma University, he had a stint with the Dallas Cowboys as their head coach. No doubt Coach Switzer could coach. But he also recognized that what Coach Jimmy Johnson had left after his retirement from coaching the Dallas Cowboys was already pretty special. Not only was Coach Switzer a great coach; he was also smart enough not to screw up what Jimmie Johnson had put in place. He added to a winning culture with his own special talents. Coach Switzer has a Super Bowl ring to prove it.

I took the same approach as Coach Switzer. I knew Dr. Lockard had developed a good thing. Now I had to absorb, perform, and maintain the standards, culture, and systems he had instilled with his team. I had to add my talents to make it even better. His mentorship allowed me to mature and become the best I could be. It was the adaptation of his systems, utilizing his contacts and knowledge, and providing a standard of excellence that set me free. I was smart enough not to screw up what he had already put in place. I am so grateful for his mentorship.

Lap 18 Lesson: *There are times that I will perform dentistry for people who simply are not in a position to afford care. Because they are grateful, I often receive a gift of satisfaction in return. After I provided extensive work on a patient, she presented me with some beautiful cuff links. I love them. They have more value than what I would have received in payment. You often receive when you give.*

Today, it gives me the warm fuzzies inside to know that I can now give back as a mentor to others. I remember when I took a Dale Carnegie course years ago. We sat in a circle and went around complementing each person in our circle, expressing one of his or her positive traits or strengths. At the end of the exercise we were asked how we felt about complimenting others? It was interesting to find that we all felt better about ourselves when we complimented others. My wife insists that I remember that lesson! Often you can receive that same gift when you mentor or help others. Whether you are being mentored, or mentoring, there are remarkable rewards with both. That is the reason it becomes so important to position yourself with your team and with your colleges in a way that you can both give and receive.

> It was interesting to find that we all felt better about ourselves when we complimented others.

Lap 18 Tipping Point
Position yourself with your team and with your colleagues in a way that you can both give and receive.

You will receive **rewards in giving.**

Chapter 19
What Goes on in Vegas Stays in Vegas

We are in business to do business. Sounds simple, doesn't it? As we discuss all of the tipping points that motivate change and create meaning, I would like to reflect on the two sides of business we must inspect. There are the hearts and the smarts. There is the emotional, compassionate, relationship-based part of a business, and then there are the facts and

> There are the hearts and the smarts.

numbers that reflect profitability. You may be surprised to learn just how dependent one may be on the other.

Keep these three things in mind when it comes to selling. I contend there are three things that matter. Does it hurt? Does it look good? How much does it cost? These factors can be interpreted a little differently and apply to your business too. Stay with me just a minute . . .

> Does it hurt? Does it look good? How much does it cost?

I am a pretty big guy. Not so tall—6 feet—but I do have pretty big shoulders and a 19 ½-inch neck. If I go to a store to buy a shirt with a 19 ½-inch neck, I find the body of the shirt is really large. So, for me to wear a tie with a shirt that has a neck I can button without a body the size of a parachute, my shirts must be custom made. A boutique store made some for me. After spending almost $200 per shirt, I had a dozen shirts made that I can't wear. For some reason, the collar doesn't lie down properly. The tailor has made several attempts to correct the collar, but after twelve months of frustration, the problem has never been resolved to my satisfaction. Now remember, this is a boutique shop that specializes in custom, quality men's wear. Stay with me here.

Lap 19 Lesson: *There is a place in Texas called Babes. They make the best fried chicken on the planet earth! Last year, I took my team there for our Christmas dinner. Remember, that is a 3-hour drive. A group in Oklahoma was able to start a franchise with this great food. One year later, the Oklahoma restaurant was out of business. We visited the restaurant several times in Oklahoma. The chicken was still awesome, but the service was simply horrible. They had the smart- it was a great recipe and awesome food. But the service was so bad, they didn't get the heart. A bad experience can overshadow the best of intentions. It has to feel good.*

It was October when my son Tyler traveled with me to Las Vegas to go to the Indy car race. A few facts need to be conveyed.

First, Tyler had turned twenty-one years of age the previous August. You do the math. He had images in his little head of how he was going to conquer Las Vegas. I chuckled inside.

Second, he had heard all about Vegas, but the only other time he had been there was when he raced his kart some ten years earlier. His college classes finished at noon on Friday, and he left directly after class to meet me at the house so we could go together to the airport for our Friday-afternoon flight. We had Friday and Saturday to enjoy Las Vegas before we went to the race on Sunday. When Tyler showed up at the house to go to the airport, I couldn't help but chuckle again. He was wearing a suit. He was stylish, or so he thought. You could tell by his attitude that he thought he was a fashion statement. "What goes on in Vegas stays in Vegas," he said.

At twenty-one years of age, he can legally drink alcohol in bars, and he can gamble too. Scary. I'm not sure if he thought he was going to pick up a hooker or meet the love of his life? As we left the house, I had to tell Tyler the truth. While he was no doubt stylish, I was just not really sure exactly what style it was? You see, he was in college. I could never get him interested in shopping for clothes. So when he showed up in his suit, it was obvious he had outgrown it long before. The pants were two inches short, and he couldn't even button the waist. His jacket was much too small in the shoulders.

Just by chance, we had received in the mail a coupon to Men's Warehouse for 50 percent off. My wife gave me the coupon, and as we departed, we agreed that we would make a quick stop for a new jacket on the way to the airport. I had never shopped at a Men's Warehouse. So when we arrived, I said to a salesman named Harry, "Harry, we are on our way to the airport. We are in a rush, and I need a jacket that actually fits my son." He directed us to jackets size 42 regular, and Tyler found three jackets he loved. I suggested one for now, and maybe the other two from Santa. Finally, clothes that fit!

Next, Harry found him a shirt that fit too. Tyler wanted cuff links just like his dad's. Vegas style? So we were about to leave Men's Warehouse when Harry said, "Dr. Fling, I can't let your son leave wearing those slacks. Find a pair that fits him in the waist, and before you are finished checking out, I will have them hemmed and ready to wear." So we did just that. Tyler and I made it to the airport with time to spare, and he looked like a happening dude. Slacks, shirt, and jacket that fit and they all actually coordinated too. Not to mention we bought them for a 50 percent discount!

Do you think we have been back to Men's Warehouse since that trip? Of course we have. Since that trip I have returned to buy five suits, twelve slacks, ten shirts, one pair of shoes, two winter jackets, seven sets of cuff links and one overcoat. I have referred many new customers to Harry. Harry and Men's Warehouse brought great value to me with excellent service.

There is no doubt that I could have bought clothes from my boutique custom clothier that were of higher quality and cost. But even though I was willing to pay a higher price, and even though the Men's Warehouse products were not as customized, the convenience and

> **Remember to create experiences that are positive.**

service that Harry gave me created a higher value than my boutique clothier. He supplied what we needed, when we needed it. He made me a loyal customer for life.

Remember what I said. There are three things to keep in mind when it comes to selling: Does it hurt? Does it look good? How much does it cost? Harry made my experience painless (does it hurt?). As a matter of fact it was enjoyable. The price was right (how much does it cost?), and Tyler was stylish (does it look good?). There are the hearts and the smarts. While the logistics of what Harry was able to do for us was essential, the great feeling we experienced had just as much

Create great experiences.

meaning. My heart didn't feel so good with my boutique clothier. So remember to create experiences that are positive and appeal to the emotions in a meaningful way.

Lap 19 Tipping Point
Create experiences that are painless, that create great value, and that appeal to the emotions in a meaningful way.

Lap 20
Costs vs. Value

I still needed some custom shirts. I asked Harry if he could do that for me. I loved his response. He said, "We don't do that. It simply isn't what we do." I feel there is a valuable lesson here. Understand your business model and do what you do best. Don't be everything to everybody unless that is your specific model. Wal-Mart has taken the approach of being everything to everybody. They do that very well. The fact is, however, in order for the company to do that, it has to create an infrastructure, a culture, and support system to accomplish its business model.

> Understand your business model and do what you do best.

All too often I see people trying to be everything to everybody, yet they don't create the appropriate infrastructure to support everything. They are providers of much and the masters of nothing.

If you are going to position yourself to do it better (like the custom clothier), you must live up to the expectations. If you don't fulfill those expectations, your customers will find an alternative. Just ask me how I know. I no longer buy clothes from the custom clothier. A large selection at a moderate price with a seamstress ready to go. That is what Men's Warehouse is about for me. As far as my boutique

Give yourself a birthday
present every year.
Give away something
you don't enjoy doing!

store goes, it lost a customer for life. Even though its threads are finer, and even though it specializes in custom, quality men's wear, it didn't fulfill my expectations. It wasn't about the cost; it was about the value. It just didn't feel good. I have to find a new custom shirt maker.

Lap 20 Lesson: *Consider this: I have suggested to many of my dental clients that they give themselves a birthday present every year. And what is that present? Give away something you don't enjoy doing! For me, it is root canals. That is a procedure I simply didn't enjoy. So I decided to give myself a gift and give that procedure away. Happy birthday to me. As a result, I have more time to do the things I really enjoy doing.*

Lap 20 Tipping Point
Cost and value are not the same.
Do what you do best and fulfill expectations.

Lap 21

Warning: They May Run

et's reflect on the initial premise I had suggested. Does it hurt? Does it look good? How much does it cost? When I ask if it hurts, because I am a dentist, you probably assume that I am referring to physical pain, but I am not. Said another way: How does it make you feel? (Does it hurt?) Does it appeal to you emotionally? (Does it look good?) Is it a good value? (How much does it cost?) I ordered my custom shirts because I placed value on having something that was customized and fit well, even

> When your desire for a positive emotional experience is satisfied, you will perceive a value commensurate with the price.

though it was at a higher cost. When the company didn't fulfill my expectations, I lost trust in the process. I didn't like how the shirts looked and the process to correct the problem became painful. It simply didn't feel good.

*If your client's experience
doesn't feel good...*

...they will run.

On the other hand, I felt wonderful about the transaction at Men's Warehouse, even though it was not as customized. Whether the transaction is about a crown or a custom shirt, it needs to appeal to your client's emotions in a positive way. When your desire for a positive emotional experience is satisfied, you will perceive a value commensurate with the price.

But heed this warning. If the seller charges a higher fee for a product or service and it doesn't appeal to the client emotionally with a positive experience, and if the client doesn't perceive value in that service commensurate with the fee, the client will run! Said another way: If your client's experience doesn't feel good, or fulfill their perception of value, they will run. And why not? If they can get the same disappointing service or the same quality somewhere else at a lower price, why shouldn't they go somewhere else?

Lap 21 Lesson: *We continually have to create value in the service we provide. I am aware that my patients can go down the street and get a crown for less money. So I have to convey a culture that relays our expertise and we must educate our clients that what we do is different. That difference is reflected in everything we do, from how we answer the phone to the atmosphere at our facility. It all has to convey who we are. If I cannot demonstrate that difference, patients will find a cheaper alternative.*

Lap 21 Tipping Point
If the fee isn't commensurate with the value, your clients will run.

Lap 22
Pick Your Driving Experience

The fact is that every business or service provider has to pick his poison. In other words: you need to determine if you are going to focus on a specific niche, or if you are going to be more of a generalist and appeal to the masses. Do I want to be a Ford or a Porsche? Both are great cars, but one operates at a very different level from the other.

I am a car guy. I love fast, sexy cars. The opportunity to race my car takes me to a different emotional level. Everyone has his or her own vice. Mine is

> In other words: you need to determine if you are going to focus on a specific niche, or if you are going to be more of a generalist and appeal to the masses.

adrenaline. When I have the experience of driving my Porsche on the edge "between fast and crash," I love how that makes me feel. I have great trust in a street car that handles like a race car. (How does it make me feel?) It is a very specific type of car that can respond like a race car. I also think there are few cars as beautiful or sexy as a Porsche. (Does it appeal to me emotionally?) The aesthetics appeal to my soul, and can make me smile. I tell my wife that I love the hips on my car. I simply think it is a beautiful car. Is it a good value? No doubt I could have a car that could cost less. But the performance, aesthetics, and fulfillment of the Porsche's racing heritage are factors that combine and motivate me to buy. The car feels good; it appeals to my emotions; and it holds great value in its performance. I'm sold.

Just like Ford or Porsche, I have chosen the customer that I try to attract to my business too. When I have a new customer, I understand that I have to compete with businesses that offer lower costs. I have picked my brand. I want to give my customers individual time and attention that makes them feel good. I want to know my customers, their needs and desires. I will have photographs and albums that show pictures of the treatment we have provided for other customers. I want my customers to see and experience our quality and know how it can look. I want to appeal to their sense of emotion and their feelings in a positive way. Lastly, I will converse about our philosophy of care. By expressing and showing patients that what and how I do something is different from the norm, I am attempting to express my brand and our value. I choose to offer a more specialized product, much like a Porsche. Not that it is better; it is simply a choice that fits my fearless clarity. All that I do focuses on building value for our brand. If our cost is more than that of the competition, I have to create value so customers feel good about their experience and the product that we deliver.

> ## There is a difference between cost and value.

Our message has to be consistent. We have to create the marketplace by the fulfilling the experience we provide to our customers.

Living a brand that is developed from your **fearless clarity** *can inspire a* **limitless spirit.**

There is a difference between cost and value. Not all drivers want the same type of car. Our job is to learn our clients' driving style and be clear on the type of car we choose to build so we can give our customers a positive driving experience.

Lap 22 Lesson: *I just love doing what I do. I have chosen a specific level of care I provide to my client. When I am treating a difficult, intense, and demanding case, I am "in the zone." That is the place where my internal juices get going. Remember the reason why developing and living your specific brand becomes so important. Living that brand that is developed from your fearless clarity inspires a spirit that can have unlimited boundaries and potential.*

And here is the reason why developing and living your specific brand becomes so important. Living the brand that is developed from your fearless clarity inspires a spirit that can have unlimited boundaries and potential.

Lap 22 Tipping Point

Develop your brand and focus on building value for your brand.

Living that brand can inspire a spirit that can have unlimited boundaries.

Chapter 23
Kindle Your Spirit

As I mentioned earlier, my son, Tyler, was diagnosed in first grade with a learning difference called a digit span problem. My understanding is that, neurologically, this affects his ability to process letters into words, words into sentences, and sentences into paragraphs. The neurological process doesn't work for him as it does for most of us.

Don't get me wrong. He is in college now and doing well, and he has learned to compensate. He is a bright young man with great potential. When he was in first grade, we placed him in a small school where he could receive special learning skills and personalized attention. He progressed to middle school where his class size averaged eight kids. This school was great for personalized learning but not so good for socializing. His small school typically fed into a larger private high school. This high school had a "reach program" offering continued support. There were about 1000 kids in the high school, and when Tyler showed up there on his first day, he only knew three or four other kids. If it wasn't overwhelming for him, it surely was for his parents!

Lap 23 Lesson: *I was worried that Tyler wanted to play football simply because he had heard about my days of playing the sport. As it turns out, his decision to play was even more bold. He did it to meet friends. He wanted to connect socially with a group he didn't know, and football provided that opportunity and gave him a sense of inclusion. In turn, football exploited his strengths, not as an athlete but as a teammate. It was making an intentional choice that allowed him to contribute his spirit to the team.*

Just after the beginning of his freshman year, Tyler approached me to say he wanted to play football. I was a little puzzled and concerned as he wasn't the biggest kid on the block, and he had never played football before. This school had some remarkable athletes with a very established program. Nonetheless, he played on the high-school team for four years. He was always there. He would be one of the first players to arrive and one of the last to leave. As a matter of fact, his team did very well. They had an average win of 36 points. They were 28–0 in a two-year period and 38–3 in a three-year period. The team was a state championship runner up, and twice won a state championship.

> In his four years of playing ball, he got on the field in a game for a total of only four plays.

This is probably where you expect me to tell you that Tyler was a star and that he went on to greatness. In my eyes he did. You see, Tyler wasn't the fastest, the strongest, or the most talented. As a matter of fact, just the opposite was true. His biggest contribution on game day was the encouragement he gave his teammates. He was the one on the sidelines high-fiving the other players and encouraging them with his

Kindle your spirit so you can be at your best.

passion. In his four years of playing ball, he got on the field in a game for a total of only four plays. That averages one play per year.

Now I don't know about you, but I would have been ready to throw in the towel. Think about it, playing on a team that wins, on average, by 36 points, and you still don't get a chance to play a down! I believe the coach did a huge injustice to many of the kids who practiced and contributed just as hard as Tyler. I don't think the coach understood what playing just one down would mean to a young man's ego. I don't think he ever considered how his actions might affect the spirit of those around him.

I stayed quiet as a parent (something I don't do well). But if I ever get a chance to tell that coach what I really think of him . . . I must say I wasn't sad when I heard he resigned from his position. But through it all, there is the thing that still amazes me. It is the spirit in my son. I believe that the disappointment and pain from never playing only made him stronger. You see, he would never miss a practice. He was the most enthusiastic player on the sidelines, always there to encourage his teammates and cheer them on. He never gave up on his team. He believed. And when the team failed, he would be the guy on the sidelines with tears in his eyes. That time was a growing experience for both of us. To his credit, he found a way to turn a weakness into strength. While he couldn't contribute with his athletic skills, he added to the team in his own way.

Place each player in a position where their gifts can benefit the team.

His spirit of encouragement, of duty and passion for his teammates, was amazing. He connected with his team in his own way, and he played his part by contributing with his unique passion and spirit. It wasn't in his physical play on the field where he made his largest contribution to his team. It was his spirit that added to the team. Just being a part of that team was meaningful to Tyler even though he never played. Remember, we all add to our team with our unique and special gifts. Recognize each players special gifts and be careful to place each player in a position where their gifts can benefit the team.

Lap 23 Tipping Point
Allow people to add to your life with their unique gifts and spirit.

Lap 24

How Do You Mend a Broken Heart?

To this day Tyler carries those same qualities of spirit and passion in life. My hope is that his enthusiasm, his passion, and a sensitive heart will be the qualities that allow him to succeed. Sometimes it is those hard lessons in life, when things don't go our way, that makes us stronger in the end. Tyler has become a stronger, more resilient person because he didn't get to play. Maybe I should thank his coach? I think I'll pass for now. I can tell you that when we experienced the times he was overlooked to play, we all experienced sorrow and frustration. The reality is that we have days when our spirit may seem broken. There are those days when our heart is simply sad. So how do you mend a broken heart? I want to share a story that may change your outlook when you are down and your spirit is low.

I received a phone call one day from a good friend. He was in tears as he asked me what I would do if I received a call like the one he had just received? His twenty-one-year-old daughter called on someone else's mobile phone from a bathroom in a Home Depot store, asking for money. She had nowhere to live; she had no money for personal necessities. On the advice he had previously received from his counselor, he had to tell her he couldn't help. After she had left rehabilitation for the second time, he had to leave it to her to rescue herself. His counselor had advised him to stop saving her, and told him to let her hit rock bottom in the hope that she would recognize the need to change and find her own way back up. His spirit was broken. Let me share with you what he did to help mend his broken heart.

As a business owner, he would often stop at a Wal-Mart store early in the morning to pick up supplies before he went in to his work. He would often see a particular older lady at the check-out counter. She was a soured woman who could seem rude and unhappy. As he went to the store the morning after he had had the conversation with his homeless daughter, he shopped with a heavy heart and a deflated spirit.

Something inspired him, though. After completing his shopping, he passed the refrigerated flower section. He decided to purchase a dozen roses. When he checked out at the counter with the unhappy clerk, he changed the spirit of two lives. He paid for his goods and as he left, he gave the roses to the clerk. "These are for you. I hope it makes your day better."

Lap 24 Lesson: *My wife and I have started something that is fun. If we are out to eat and we see a serviceman or service woman, we anonymously buy their meal. We were at a Cheesecake Factory the first time we did this. Ahead of us were two servicemen. We asked the waitress to send us their bill. She did so and asked, "Who may I tell them bought their meal?" I replied, "Don't tell them anything." As we were leaving after our dinner, the two service men left too. We heard them talk as they walked across the parking lot, wondering who had bought their meal. I had a warm fuzzy. My spirit was elevated.*

Mend your broken heart by giving your gifts.

She started to cry. She said, "No one has ever done anything like that for me before."

After that day, he and the clerk have their own special bond. Her spirit was elevated by an act of kindness. But a surprising thing happened to my friend. He found that by helping her, his spirit was elevated too. He started to mend his broken heart. There is great receiving in giving.

I believe that this is why Tyler carries the spirit that he does. Supporting his team and encouraging each player elevated his own

My point is you must find your own way to give back and you may find that what you get in return is even greater.

spirit. I can't tell you how proud I would be to get a picture of Tyler after each game. He displayed so much pride and passion you would have thought he had scored the winning touchdown.

My point is you must find your own way to give back and you may find that what you get in return is even greater.

Lap 24 Tipping Point
When your spirit is down, find a way to give back and you will find that your spirit will be elevated.

Lap 25
Finding the Catalyst

You will recall in the movie *City Slickers* that Curlee asked Mitch, "What is the secret to life?" Curlee continued, while holding up one finger, "This one thing. Stick to that one thing and you will figure it out." Mitch asked, "What is that one thing?" Curlee said, "That is for you to figure out."

As we have discussed, there are a multitude of reasons why someone may not have the catalyst for change. They may lack a fearless clarity; they may not have the drive or passion; they may not have the team or systems in place to apply what they already know; or they may lack the spirit to make change. I contend there is a bigger piece that needs to be put in place to solve the puzzle for positive change. It is that one thing.

Remember what I said in Lap 1: I had to develop a new fearless clarity. For me, the catalyst to swim thirty-two laps was having the clear vision of a healthier me. But what is the one thing that creates that clarity for me so that I can reach my goal?

Recall this from before. It was the fall of 2010 when I was motivated to get in better shape. This is not to say that I was grossly overweight or out of shape; I wasn't. But I now had the motivation to do more. I don't remember how, but I was exposed to swimming. I had never done much swimming and as I began my efforts, I felt defeated when, at my first attempt, I was able to swim only one and a half laps. I wondered how I would ever complete the thirty-two laps that made a mile. I knew how to swim. But doing it for an entire mile, that was another story. It wasn't that I didn't know how to swim a mile. There was something far greater that motivated me to swim.

It was a Friday, the week after Thanksgiving, when I got a call from my physician. After almost two years of hormonal therapy and test results that were very irregular, my physician called to tell me, "You don't have to go to the hospital today, but I want you there Monday. I think you may have a brain tumor." My world was turned upside down. This couldn't be happening to me. And exactly what did that mean? Cancer, surgery, no more work? I was lost. It couldn't happen to me!

Well, it did. As it turns out, he was correct. And for various reasons it wasn't going to be until June that my surgery would be performed. I had six months with time to ponder all of the possibilities. And ponder I did. I did have the surgery in June and it all went remarkably well. As it turns out, I had a noncancerous, growth hormone producing, pituitary tumor. That was the reason that my hormone levels were so irregular. The great news? It wasn't cancer. I want to be very clear that I am not a cancer survivor. I don't want to suggest that what I endured approached that level. Trust me when I say that there are a great many other people who have had to endure much more than I have.

As I mentioned, after the diagnosis was confirmed, I had a six-month wait before my surgery. All kinds of things go through your mind at a time like this. I sometimes seemed to want to think the worst. The wait gave me time to reflect on many things, some of which I had never given thought to before, such as death. Not that I ever felt threatened by death; I didn't. And the physicians were almost certain it was not a cancerous tumor. Nonetheless, I considered the worst, and I prayed for the best. The tumor gave me a very different perspective on life. And this experience reveals that one thing that really is the secret, that one thing that creates that catalyst for change: **Significance.**

Lap 25 Lesson: *A patient needed to have her teeth reconstructed before her daughter's wedding in ten months. She had significant tooth destruction because she sucked on lemons. The acid had damaged the teeth badly. It was a difficult reconstruction, but we accomplished the task in time for the wedding. She loved her new smile, so much so that she hired a photographer to take some beautiful portraits. Now let me tell you the rest of the story. She was in a wheel chair. This made her treatment even more difficult. Nonetheless we got it completed. One day when I was working in my lab, Tammy tapped me on the shoulder and asked me to step in the doorway. I reluctantly did. As I looked down the hallway, I saw our patient sitting in her wheelchair. She stood up, walked down the hallway, and gave me a hug. Did her teeth make her walk? Of course not. Her new smile elevated her self-esteem to a level that motivated her to walk. We all have a unique gift of significance.*

I was suddenly motivated to get in better physical condition after my initial diagnosis. It was important that my body was in the best possible physical shape before surgery. That had enough significance to motivate me to change. So I swam. And as I swam, I learned that working my way up to one mile—thirty-two laps—wouldn't be easy. But I had a fearless clarity to achieve that goal. I had the motivation to complete that task. I used a great system with techniques that

*The one thing that creates a catalyst
for change is finding...*

...significance.

allowed me to succeed, and I had my coach to mentor and advise me along the way. These events revealed to me that the real key to change is understanding the significance that change will have in our life and the effect that change has on the lives we touch. Significance is the one thing that can be the catalyst for change!

Lap 25 Tipping Point
Significance is the primary
catalyst for change.

Lap 26
Don't Swim Alone

As I would swim my laps, often I would lose track of which lap I was swimming. I had to find a way to keep track. So I got two Tupperware containers. In one of them I placed thirty-two beads. Each bead represented one lap. As I completed each lap, I transferred one bead from one container into the other container. When all the beads were transferred, I had completed one mile.

As I would swim a lap, I started to place meaning on every bead I transferred. Every time I took a bead from one container and put it in the other, I would reflect on a memory: my wedding, a child being born, a ski trip, or racing the car. I would reflect on things that had meaning for my spirit. These memories inspired me to push.

And then I made another important observation. As I stopped to transfer my bead

This was a reminder that everyone else has his or her own set of unique circumstances to consider too.

from one to the other container, I would look down the other lanes at the pool and see all of the other swimmers. There were eleven other lanes with swimmers swimming their own races. They were tracking their laps too. You see I was not the only one with beads to transfer. Often I get caught up in focusing on only my own circumstances. This was a reminder that everyone else has his or her own set of unique circumstances to consider too. They have their beads to monitor. So look down the other lanes and consider others have their circumstances too. And be aware that you may help others in their journey. Even during times that challenge our spirit, be aware that other people's circumstances may have great significance too. Remember that, often, you can elevate your spirit by helping others even when you both are in times of need.

Lap 26 Lesson: *It was at the time of my diagnosis that my son's best friend was diagnosed with Hodgkin's lymphoma at the early age of twenty. No doubt he and his family had so much more to consider than I. They are both in the dental profession and they are remarkable people. He has undergone all of his treatment and now he is doing great! I had the honor to write a letter of recommendation for his application to dental school. This is a young man who lives with a fearless clarity. My point is that the people around us have issues of which we may be unaware when our world is spinning out of control. So don't swim alone because the person next to you may need help too.*

Lap 26 Tipping Point
During times that challenge our spirit, be aware that other people's circumstances may have great significance too.

Lap 27

Don't Live in Fear

*L*et me give you something else to consider. Remember that as I would swim, I would transfer a bead from one container to the other to track my progress. The events that had transpired made me keenly aware of another consideration. Every time I transfer a bead, I was closer to reaching my goal. With that transfer goes a memory or a life event. Remember, though, that for every bead I transfer into the one container, I have taken a bead out of the other container. And one day, I will find that I am completely out of beads; the one container is empty. There are no more beads to transfer.

I think back to when my kids were babies. The fact is that we get about sixteen summers with our kids before they are gone. Once the driver's license is earned, they find their wings. We look up and the beads are gone. We never know when our beads of life will run out either. Someday can be too late. I don't tell you that so that you'll live in fear. I tell you that so that you will live with *significance*. I believe that significance is the link between knowing and doing. Finding your significance in whatever you do is that one thing that can create change.

> I believe that significance is the link between knowing and doing.

Don't live in fear,

live in Significance.

Lap 27 Lesson: *We have had the good fortune to have my wife's parents travel with us to most of our race events. They love watching and being a part of it with us. Time has passed and those days are gone. I don't convey that in sadness, but rather, I remember those times with gratitude. The glass isn't half empty; it is half full because we will always have those memories together. The part they played in the lives of our children and our lives has remarkable significance. So live with intention and appreciate the significance of the smallest of gifts.*

Dr. L. D. Pankey once said, "I never saw a tooth walk into my office." My significance is not just the fact that I fix someone's tooth. It is what that does for that person's spirit and self-esteem. It is what that experience does for that person, for my team, and even for me. Whether you are a brain surgeon, a parent, a janitor, or a hamburger maker, understand the significance of the role you can play in someone else's world. Understand how sharing your gift with others allows you and those other people to grow their spirit. And know that now is your time to make a difference.

Lap 27 Tipping Point
One day your beads will be gone. So, don't live in fear. Live with significance.

Gather Ye Rosebuds

R ejoice in your memories, dream for tomorrow, but live for today because someday can be too late. I love this poem that points out just how important it is to live in the now, for it may be too late tomorrow.

Gather ye rosebuds while ye may,
Old Time is still a-flying:
And this same flower that smiles today
Tomorrow will be dying.
The glorious lamp of heaven, the sun,
The higher he's a-getting,
The sooner will his race be run,
And nearer he's to setting.
That age is best which is the first,
When youth and blood are warmer;
But being spent, the worse, and worst
Times still succeed the former.
Then be not coy, but use your time,
And while ye may, go marry:
For having lost but once your prime,
You may for ever tarry.

—Robert Herrick

The point is that now is the best time to contribute your gifts. Often it is not until it is too late that we try to offer our gift to others.

> ## Lap 28 Tipping Point
> Rejoice in your memories, dream for tomorrow, but live for today. Now is the best time to contribute your gifts.

Rejoice in your memories,

Dream for tomorrow, but

Live for today.

Lap 29
Iwo Jima

Many times, remarkable experiences are waiting for us to realize them. Take the time to seize the moment. I recently had a patient come in to my office to have his teeth cleaned. I have known him for more than twenty-two years. He is in his early nineties. I have treated him through many life events including his losing his son. I still get goose bumps when I think about his recent appointment. After my hygienists cleaned his teeth, I examined him and found two small areas of root decay. He wasn't in the mood to have them fixed that day, but I knew how difficult it was for him to get out of the house to make it back to my office. I wanted to save him another trip. I asked him when his birthday was. He said it was in about one month.

I said, "John, I want to give you an early birthday present. I want to fix your teeth today. That way you won't have to make an extra trip. And it's on me. Let's call it an early birthday present."

To my surprise he said okay. So I fixed his teeth that day. But I will tell you that on that day I received a bigger gift from him than he did from me.

After we were finished, I made small talk and asked him about a TV show I had recently seen, called *WWII in HD*. My son and I are

WWII buffs. I also knew that, given John's age, he probably had been involved in WWII. The makers of *WWII in HD* had searched the globe for two years to find color footage of different WWII battles that had never been seen on TV before. I told him how intrigued I was with WWII, and how I was surprised to learn from this show that there were more Americans killed in the invasion of Iwo Jima than in the invasion of Normandy on D-day. After I mentioned that surprising fact, he gave me a deeply thoughtful look and said, "Yes I know. I was there."

Touch a spirit.

I was dumbfounded. I touched his arm and said, "Thank you."

This large, opinionated, rough-edged man started to tell me stories. He told me about his friend who was trapped on the island in a battle. While telling this story, he had to stop and compose himself and breathe deeply. He sat there motionless and then began to cry.

He said, "I haven't talked about that very much. I didn't know it would be so hard."

He spoke with pauses. He had to stop in an attempt to express his thoughts without shedding tears. The emotion of the moment was extraordinary. You could see him traveling back in time through the emotional memory of one of the most significant events of his life.

We decided to change the subject and move on, but as he departed that day, I said, "John, this may sound a little crazy coming from your dentist, but we love you." Once again he cried. The next day, I sent him a bouquet of flowers with a note that said, "Thank you." Spirits were touched.

For me, seizing the moment was taking the time to talk to John. It wasn't about his teeth. It was about our relationship and our experience. It was about the significance of the moment. Remarkable experiences are waiting to be realized, but we have to take the time to recognize them. Those moments can be powerful. For John, that day on Iwo Jima had remarkable significance. Not just the significance of changing the course of the world but significance on a more personal level. Dying for freedom was of real significance for him. As a soldier, he knew what had to be accomplished. But invading the beach and possibly dying was a real consequence. What he *had to do* was very different from what he *wanted to do*. The catalyst for bridging the gap between knowing and doing was the significance of the moment.

> First identify the significance of what you are doing because that is the primary factor that can motivate change.

Lap 29 Lesson: *There is a remarkable lesson in the gift I received. By taking time and interest to talk with John, to seize the moment, to take the time to listen to him, I learned some things about him that allowed us to make a personal connection that otherwise I would not have known. By making that connection with John, by learning his story, I was able to connect with him at a more significant level.*

My point is that developing that relationship with John was what was most significant. The bottom line is this: when you have things to do, first identify the significance of what you are doing because that is the primary factor that can motivate change. Finding a personal connection can reveal significance that you never knew existed.

Lap 29 Tipping Point
Remarkable experiences are waiting for us.
There is significance in finding
a personal connection.

Lap 30

Rudder or Elevator?

ave you ever had a client who has been so rude to your team that they wished he would take his business elsewhere? I had just such a person in my practice. This large, deep-voiced, older man intimidated me. As a matter of fact, one of my hygienists said she didn't want to see him anymore because he was too rude.

On one of his appointments, as I visited with him, I talked with him about various things. I told him that my wife and I had just returned from a trip in our airplane. He asked what kind of airplane I had. I told him it was a Cessna Turbo 210. He then told me that he also had a 210! I asked him if he had ever been to a QB meeting. QB is a pilot organization that I had been a part of for several years. We even have our own secret handshake—not really! He chuckled and said he had been a QB for more than twenty-five years. I asked him why I had never seen him at a meeting and invited him to join me at the next one.

Our next QB meeting was held the following Monday night, and guess who showed up? We enjoyed dinner together and after the meeting we went on our way. It was some three months later when he returned to my office to have his teeth cleaned. At the end of that day, my hygienist came into my office and asked what in the world had happened to make her grumpy patient so nice? He was a different person. It was as though she had a new best friend.

Lap 30 Lesson: *The power of personal connection is amazing. Because my patient and I had found something we both loved and had in common, our relationship was much more enjoyable. He approached me and my team with a different attitude.*

A few years later I learned that his granddaughter was about to graduate from dental school. She was going to practice in Oklahoma City. Knowing this, I fully expected him to transfer his dental care to her practice. Sure enough, one day my office received a call requesting his wife's records. My assumption was that he would transfer too. Again, to my surprise, I came into the office one day to see he was on the schedule. He was there to have his teeth cleaned. At the end of the day my hygienist came into my office and she commented on just how much he had changed. When I completed my examination that day, I explained to him that I was a little puzzled. I asked him, "What are you doing here? I figured you would see your granddaughter for your dental care." He replied, "Oh I would, but she doesn't know a rudder from an elevator."

By finding something in common, we were able to gain a different level of trust, and he treated us with a completely different attitude. You can see the importance of taking the time to develop a relationship. Building trust and finding connection is remarkably significant.

Lap 30 Tipping Point
Develop a personal connection by finding something in common.
Building trust is significant.

*The power
of personal
connection is
amazing.*

Lap 31

Look Inside

My wife and daughter are horse nuts. As a matter of fact, I have accused my wife of having an affair. It just happens to be with a horse! My daughter Kinsey has shown her horse on a national level for many years. In 2009 she was the High Point All Around International Champion for girls in the ten-to-thirteen age group.

Now, four years later, she just completed the International show again. This year her results were not as successful. I explained to her something that is remarkably important. The results of her show don't define who she is. The difference between first and third place is a different-color ribbon. Instead, who she is will define how she prepares

> Too many times we allow what we do to define who we are. Instead, who we are defines what we do.

and how she reacts to adversity and disappointment. Too many times we allow what we do to define who we are. Instead, who we are defines what we do. Let me share another story with you that will demonstrate the lesson I conveyed to her.

This past year I had the honor to give the eulogy at my father-in-law's funeral. It was a remarkable ceremony, not because I gave the eulogy but because of his legacy to and his significance in Oklahoma history and in so many lives.

On what has been described as the darkest day in the history of the Oklahoma Highway Patrol—May 26, 1978—three troopers were killed in two separate shootouts with two escaped Oklahoma State Prison convicts. The three troopers killed were Trooper Houston "Pappy" Summers, Trooper Billy Young, and Lt. Pat Grimes. My father-in-law, Lt. Hoyt Hughes and Pat were partners who had drawn an assignment to search for the escapees.

Trooper Summers and Young were found dead on a county road following a shootout with the two escapees. The convicts had stolen a farmer's pickup truck and weapons and later encountered the two troopers. Following the exchange of gunfire that mortally wounded both Summers and Young, the escapees sped in the stolen pickup truck into a small town, setting up an ambush point in a brushy area in a residential sector.

As Lt. Grimes and my father-in-law cruised through the residential area, seeking the convicts, they were fired upon in the pair's ambush, and Lt. Grimes suffered fatal wounds. Hoyt was hit in the shoulder and arm.

Hoyt stepped out of his cruiser and fired point-blank at the hidden escapees. Despite his wounds he was able to put an end to one of the two convicts. A few seconds later, Lt. Mike Williams fatally wounded the second convict, bringing an end to a thirty-four-day trail of terror. The two convicts had been sought in a six-state flight to Alabama and back to Oklahoma, following their tunneling out of the state prison at McAlester. In addition to the three OHP troopers, the escaped convicts killed five other people, and three others were wounded.

Lap 31 Lesson: *While Kinsey was down about the results of her latest placing at the international horse show, she learned a great lesson. The results of that show do not make her who she is. Instead, who she is will determine how she prepares for, and how she reacts to adversity. We can't always win at everything. But we can allow who we are to affect how we react. That is more important than winning.*

Some thirty-three years later, Hoyt passed away. Needless to say, many news sources and the Oklahoma Highway Patrol recognized his passing. The respect and thanks that the family received from the highway patrol and the community was overwhelming. But I feel there needs to be clarification about all of the heroes of that darkest day, including Hoyt. You see, some people may think that the events of that day and what happened to Hoyt made him the hero that he was. But I believe that is not true. Rather, it was the man he was that allowed him to act as he did that day, which, in turn, made him a hero. It wasn't the event that made Hoyt. It was Hoyt who altered the event. It was Hoyt knowing the significance of the

> Don't allow what you do to determine who you are. Allow who you are to determine what you do.

moment that motivated him to do something extraordinary while knowing the possible consequences. Those events didn't make Hoyt the man he was. The man he was affected those events. It is the significance of who he was that bridged the gap between knowing and doing and made him a hero.

You see, often in our lives we believe our value is based on what we do. My contention is that it is not in the knowing; it is in the

What you do doesn't
determine who you are.

Who you are
determines
what you do.

doing. But here is that "one thing". Base your "Doing" on the significance that adds to your "self" and to those around you. Don't allow what you do to determine who you are. Allow who you are to determine what you do.

I have relayed this story to Kinsey and she understands that the tail doesn't wag the dog. No doubt, she would rather finish first instead of last in every event she enters. But the truth is that while she is an amazing person, her being so special is not based on how she finishes. Instead, who she is affects how she prepares and reacts to positive and negative circumstances. The dog wags the tail.

Lap 31 Tipping Point
It is who we are that bridges the gap between knowing and doing. Don't allow what you do to determine who you are. Allow who you are to determine what you do.

Lap 32
A Little Hero in Us All

I pride myself in being a good father. I question whether I do it all that well, but it isn't from lack of trying. Maybe sometimes I even try too hard. I have attempted to serve as an example to my children as I know they are watching me even when I don't see them watching. My focus has been on their trying to do their best and on their knowing they are good people at their core. I have passed on many of these tipping points to my kids.

Let me share a story with you that gives a father hope. The professor of Tyler's summer course asked his students to name their heroes. Tyler volunteered to answer. His answer may surprise you. His hero wasn't whom you might think. It wasn't a sports figure and it wasn't even his dad. His answer? He said his hero was himself! He explained that since his learning issues in first grade, he knew how hard it would be to make it through school, much less college. He was his own hero for managing a difficult challenge.

I can't help but be proud of him. I know that, as a father and a mentor, one of the greatest gifts I can give my children is the gift of self-esteem. I have often heard that our strengths are our weaknesses, and our weaknesses, our strengths. While Tyler's learning issues have been his weakness, they have made his core stronger. The point to consider is that often our mentors are not just our peers but may be people who are much younger than us.

Lap 32 Lesson: *After the collapse of the towers on 9/11, it became apparent that the only way out of lower Manhattan was from the harbor. Ferries were working to capacity, but there weren't enough resources to complete the evacuation of masses of people. While they were attempting to rescue the stranded New Yorkers, they had no idea if there would be other attacks and they even wondered if their boats would become targets. When the towers collapsed, the city came to a complete stop. Obviously there was mass chaos and no way to escape. They needed more help. So the coast guard made a call for any boat willing to help to meet at Governors Island. Within one hour, hundreds of private and company boats arrived. They were small and large. Together they organized to complete the biggest naval evacuation since WWII when over 339,000 French and British soldiers were evacuated from Dunkirk. On 9/11, hundreds of boats organized to rescue and evacuate almost 500,000 people in only nine hours! Ordinary people doing extraordinary things. Their significance has added to the well-being and safety of thousands of people. There is a little hero inside all of us.*

So don't be surprised if you can teach your peers a thing or two, and don't be afraid to learn from younger people. I have learned from

> ## Don't be surprised if you can teach your peers a thing or two, and don't be afraid to learn from younger people.

my son and my daughter. Mentorship can occur in ways you may not expect. Tyler and Kinsey are heroes in my life.

Recognize that we all have our special gifts to

There is a little hero inside all of us.

offer. We all have a little hero inside each one of us. No matter if that hero is a Highway Patrolman or a college student, or an equestrian champion. The important thing is to find your significance.

Lap 32 Tipping Point

Don't be surprised if you can teach your peers a thing or two, and don't be afraid to learn from young people.

There is a little hero inside all of us.

Be a hero in your own special way.

Swim Your Own Race

*T*hink about two ends of the spectrum. At one end is what I call the "Living of Life." This includes the things that occupy our everyday existence: Get the kids to school. Is the schedule full? Wash the car. When are we going on vacation? My assistant is sick. Dinner at 6. How are your grades? Is the crown back from the lab? Are we going to have enough money to retire? This end of the spectrum is full of pressure. It is very competitive. If we don't grade out as well as others, then we are a failure. We are judged on how we did in relation to others. Our success is based upon what we impose on our "self."

At the other end of the spectrum is what I call "Life of Living." This refers to the idea that what or how we do something isn't as important as why we do it. It is not based upon how we did in relation to others. It doesn't impose a competitive pressure, thus it relieves us of such pressure. Instead, it asks us to impose the significance of what we do for ourselves or for others.

It was 1985, just after I graduated dental school, that I started flying lessons. I had always wanted to fly. I can remember, as a young kid living only blocks away from an airport, I was always fascinated with airplanes. So I pursued my dream.

While taking ground school, I met Drew and his wife, Kathy. We became great friends, and we even went on to buy an airplane together. As we became more accomplished with our flying, we took aerobatic lessons so we could learn how to do the really fun stuff. Then, one day, I got a call you never want to receive. Drew had been practicing his aerobatic routine when he crashed and was killed. All of us were devastated.

Beyond the expected grief and sadness, I had to ponder the continuation of my flying hobby. Was it safe? Could that happen to my family and me? What about flying at night, and what about flying in instrument conditions? All of these things had some level of risk. Should I find something else to do? Should I be fearful of all the possible ramifications and give up one of the things I really loved to do?

I still remember the morning of April 19, 1995. I was working on a patient in my back treatment room. I sat next to a large picture window. As I worked, I heard a large rumble and I felt the glass shake. I didn't know what had happened, but I knew it was something big. I still don't know why, but I looked at the clock. I commented to Tammy, "It is 9:02."

It was a few minutes later that another one of my team members interrupted us to say, "The Murrah building in downtown Oklahoma City has had a bomb explode outside."

We had no idea that it would turn out to be so devastating. It would remain the most destructive act of terrorism on American soil until the September 11, 2001, attack. The Oklahoma blast claimed 168 lives, and injured more than 680 people. The blast destroyed or damaged 324 buildings within a sixteen-block radius, destroyed or burned 86 cars, and shattered glass in 258 nearby buildings. We had friends, neighbors, and patients who were affected by this act of terrorism. The people who died in the Murrah bombing didn't get to choose that day. They just happened to be in the wrong place at the wrong time. But they definitely didn't get to choose.

My point? We are not the ones who choose when we die. But we can choose how we live. Maybe Drew could have controlled his destiny, or could he? Should his tragedy keep me from living my life? There were 168 people who had no control that day in Oklahoma City. So keep the message close to your heart. **Do what you love, but don't be blind. And by all means, don't live in fear. Live your life with a fearless clarity and with a spirit that creates significance. If you do that, then, when your destiny is fulfilled, you will have made the world a better place.**

> We are not the ones who choose when we die. But we can choose how we live.

Change is not easy. Consider your thirty-two laps and know that finding your significance can bridge the gap between knowing and doing. I hope you will find that one thing that can move your spirit and motivate you to meaningful change. I believe it is your spirit and the significance that you give to yourself and others that motivates change. Live life like a hero because you are a hero.

Thirty-two really isn't mystic. It is just the number of laps that makes a mile. It is the number of teeth I treat every day. It is the number of tipping points that have revealed themselves to me. It is as Michelangelo said, "Every piece of granite has a beautiful statue inside it. It only takes a person with a vision, a passion, a hammer, and a chisel to remove the excess granite to reveal that beautiful sculpture inside."

Thirty-two has a connection with my soul. I hope you too will learn why completing your thirty-two laps has meaning. I hope you find your significance in the smallest of places, because those are the forces that make the world go around.

We are not the ones who
choose when we die.
But we can choose
how we live.

How can you use this book?

MOTIVATE

EDUCATE

THANK

INSPIRE

PROMOTE

CONNECT

Why have a custom version of *32 Laps*?

- Build personal bonds with customers, prospects, employees, donors, and key constituencies
- Develop a long-lasting reminder of your event, milestone, or celebration
- Provide a keepsake that inspires change in behavior and change in lives
- Deliver the ultimate "thank you" gift that remains on coffee tables and bookshelves
- Generate the "wow" factor

Books are thoughtful gifts that provide a genuine sentiment that other promotional items cannot express. They promote employee discussions and interaction, reinforce an event's meaning or location, and they make a lasting impression. Use your book to say "Thank You" and show people that you care.

32 Laps is available in bulk quantities and in customized versions at special discounts for corporate, institutional, and educational purposes. To learn more please contact our Special Sales team at:

1.866.775.1696 • sales@advantageww.com • www.AdvantageSpecialSales.com